T0323699

Cambridge Elements

Elements in Political Economy
edited by
David Stasavage
New York University

THE PUZZLE OF CLIENTELISM

Political Discretion and Elections Around the World

Miriam A. Golden
European University Institute

Eugenia Nazrullaeva
London School of Economics

CAMBRIDGE
UNIVERSITY PRESS

Shaftesbury Road, Cambridge CB2 8EA, United Kingdom

One Liberty Plaza, 20th Floor, New York, NY 10006, USA

477 Williamstown Road, Port Melbourne, VIC 3207, Australia

314–321, 3rd Floor, Plot 3, Splendor Forum, Jasola District Centre, New Delhi – 110025, India

103 Penang Road, #05–06/07, Visioncrest Commercial, Singapore 238467

Cambridge University Press is part of Cambridge University Press & Assessment, a department of the University of Cambridge.

We share the University's mission to contribute to society through the pursuit of education, learning and research at the highest international levels of excellence.

www.cambridge.org
Information on this title: www.cambridge.org/9781009323215
DOI: 10.1017/9781009323208

First published 2023

A catalogue record for this publication is available from the British Library.

ISBN 978-1-009-32321-5 Paperback
ISSN 2398-4031 (online)
ISSN 2514-3816 (print)

Additional resources for this publication at www.cambridge.org/Golden_Online appendix.

The Puzzle of Clientelism
Political Discretion and Elections Around the World

Elements in Political Economy

DOI: 10.1017/9781009323208
First published online: January 2023

Miriam A. Golden
European University Institute

Eugenia Nazrullaeva
London School of Economics

Author for correspondence: Miriam A. Golden, miriam.golden@eui.eu

Abstract: This Element presents newly collected cross-national data on reelection rates of lower house national legislators from almost 100 democracies around the world. Reelection rates are low/high in countries where clientelism and vote buying are high/low. Drawing on theory developed to study lobbying, the authors explain why politicians continue clientelist activities although they do not secure reelection. The Element also provides a thorough review of the last decade of literature on clientelism, which the authors define as discretionary resource distribution by political actors. The combination of novel empirical data and theoretically grounded analysis provides a radically new perspective on clientelism. Finally, the Element suggests that clientelism evolves with economic development, assuming new forms in highly developed democracies but never entirely disappearing.

Keywords: clientelism, patronage, economic development, elections, reelection

JEL classifications: D72, D73, H11, H41, H42, K16, K42, 057

ISBNs: 9781009323215 (PB), 9781009323208 (OC)
ISSNs: 2398-4031 (online), 2514-3816 (print)

Contents

Further online supplementary material can be accessed at www.cambridge.org/Golden_Online appendix

1 Introduction

Recent years have witnessed an abundance of studies about the operations of political parties, election campaigns, and on-the-ground politics in less developed democracies. Many of these studies are framed using the notion of clientelism, considered a signature feature of political processes in less developed countries (Kitschelt & Wilkinson, 2007). Why does clientelism attract so much attention? Or perhaps we might ask: Why has clientelism become a standard term of abuse held responsible for all manner of democratic defects in poor countries?

The clientelist phenomenon invokes at least three prominent normative narratives. Clientelism breaches democratic norms of equal consideration of all citizens (Scanlon, 2018). In clientelist settings, politicians cater to groups and individuals rather than seeking to improve the general welfare; accordingly, they undertake transfers to small groups and individuals rather than writing legislation to better the fortunes of large swathes of the electorate. Particularistic and personalistic ties replace concern on the part of political representatives for the public good. Second, clientelistic politicians are typically depicted as deliberately targeting voters strictly in exchange for electoral support. Citizens who provide the highest electoral benefits – rather than those most in need or most deserving, according to universalistic criteria – become recipients of public resources. Finally, clientelism creates hierarchies, in which dependent voters are at the bottom and politicians at the top. This dependency allows the latter to act in their own interests with impunity. Clientelism thereby distorts links in the accountability chain between voters and representatives (Stokes et al., 2013, ch. 9; also Fox, 2015). Voters are clients instead of citizens (cf. Fox, 1994).

The quantitative importance of clientelism as an organizing concept in poor democracies – and even in democratic regimes more broadly – is reflected in the results of a Google Scholar search (conducted in August 2021), which shows that approximately 30,300 academic articles and books have been written on the topic since 2001, including 25,200 since 2011 alone. This is vastly greater than the 8,430 scholarly contributions that Google Scholar reports were produced in the two decades between 1980 and 2000. Within political science, more than a dozen books and scores of articles have been published within the last decade on the topic of clientelism – and many more if we extend our purview to encompass economics, anthropology, and sociology.

But what precisely is clientelism? We define it as *the discretionary use by politicians of resources for electoral purposes.*[1] Our definition highlights

---

[1] We thank Stephane Wolton for his help elaborating this conceptualization of clientelism.

what we see as clientelism's two distinguishing features: *discretion* and *electoral purpose*. Because clientelism occurs via political discretion, the processes involved are distinct from those involved in lawmaking, which obey constitutional norms and procedures. Moreover, discretion carries with it the notion of particularistic excludability: voters receive something from a politician because the politician chooses to provide it, and thus may have chosen not to. The electoral purpose of clientelism means that politicians who engage in it do not do so out of benevolence or consideration of the public interest. Instead, clientelism offers opportunities for politicians to improve their electoral fortunes. The first section of this Element is devoted to our definition. We justify it, contrast it with other definitions, and explain how we might adapt it to different situations.

We then turn to reviewing the literature on clientelism. We focus on works published or made public since 2011, since prior studies are already covered in the excellent review of Hicken (2011) (and recently extended in Hicken and Nathan [2020]). Contemporary research on clientelism has been rich and creative. It has employed a wide variety of methods, ranging from the ethnographic to the experimental, with data collection usually occurring via time-intensive field research. Much of the data so gathered have revealed previously unknown information. As a result, the recent literature, we argue, has deepened our understanding of political processes and outcomes across much of the world. As a central concept and object of empirical research in the field of comparative politics, clientelism deserves continued – but skeptical – scrutiny.

In our analysis, we follow others (notably, Nichter [2018]) and distinguish two varieties of clientelism: what we refer to as campaign and welfare clientelism. Campaign clientelism occurs during the electoral campaign, broadly conceived. It is ostensibly directed at winning votes and is practiced by challengers as well as by incumbent politicians. It can take the form of gifts of goods or cash to individuals, or subsidies and infrastructure to whole communities. It has been at the center of debates on clientelism, with many studies analyzing its goals and significance. Scholars have built on each other, sometimes critically, generating an engaging and productive debate. During the process, the literature moved from interpreting campaign clientelism as vote buying to one of turnout buying. More recent work departs from both interpretations and instead suggests campaign clientelism may be a way for candidates to signal concern for their constituents or to signal their own electoral viability. Scholars have thus collectively adapted their understanding of how campaign clientelism is interpreted on the basis of new evidence.

Although less often studied by scholars, welfare clientelism is in our opinion equally important. It consists of responses by politicians to constituents' requests for help in securing access to benefits from the state. Thanks to their privileged access to state resources, the politicians in question are usually incumbent officeholders. The sequence of activities characteristic of welfare clientelism is different from campaign clientelism. Campaign clientelism is instigated by individuals seeking public office and is directed at voters. With welfare clientelism, the interactions are reversed: an officeholder receives a request from a voter and then decides whether and how to respond. Welfare clientelism is a way for politicians to build their reputations with an eye on a future electoral contest – but their incentives to respond to requests by voters also depend on the capacity of citizens to organize and hold them accountable.

The literature has not only analyzed and tried to interpret clientelism. Some studies have also attempted to measure its electoral effectiveness, although there is disagreement about how effective clientelism is at buying votes. To more directly engage this controversy, we introduce a new dataset. We have assembled data that measures reelection rates of national legislators to lower chambers in democracies around the world. The new data are the main contribution of this Element. Our data show that reelection rates decrease with the degree of clientelism, at least as it is commonly measured across countries. In other words, the data show that countries rife with clientelism are those where the average legislator is most susceptible to defeat.

The aggregate pattern is thus inconsistent with what any standard theory of clientelism would lead us to expect. Why buy votes if not to secure reelection? To think through this problem, we contrast the macro-level pattern we have uncovered with claims arising from micro-level studies. According to the latter, where it is common, clientelism is the best electoral strategy available to candidates for public office.

But how can clientelism be the best strategy available to individual candidates for elected office and yet lead to low aggregate reelection rates? To make sense of this apparent paradox, we turn to the literature on lobbying and campaign contributions due to Grossman and Helpman (2001) and reinterpret it in relation to clientelism (cf. Coate & Morris, 1999). In this framework, special interest lobbies donate to political candidates yet donations – although normatively unpalatable to voters – do not successfully buy legislation. The reason is that the contributions from both sides of the political spectrum cancel each other out. As a result, lobbying and campaign contributions by special interest groups are inefficient but persistent. The reason for widespread and persistent campaign clientelism is similar: in competitive political environments, once one candidate resorts to vote buying, so must all others or risk electoral defeat. Thus, clientelism generates a prisoner's dilemma for politicians who engage in it.

In a similar spirit, we invoke the well-known literature on electoral account-ability (Fearon, 1999; Ferejohn, 1974) to think through the politically inef-fective strategies politicians construct when they provide assistance while in office. Here, too, attempts at distinguishing oneself as a particularly generous politician fail if voters expect and thus discount generosity. Welfare clien-telism while in public office is necessary but inconsequential for electoral success.

Our reinterpretation of clientelism highlights a perhaps underappreciated aspect of political environments that are conducive to it. As our data under-score, widespread clientelism is characteristic of *competitive* political environ-ments – competitive in the sense that the incumbent is not likely to retain his seat and public office is passed along to a series of challengers. Yet precisely because the incumbent lacks any electoral advantage, he must use all possible techniques to mobilize his followers to come to the polls, up to and includ-ing techniques that are patently illegal. Once one political party or candidate engages in clientelism, all must follow.

Because they create a prisoner's dilemma, the use of clientelistic strategies can only be reduced when some outside actor – perhaps the judiciary, perhaps a new political party – enters the arena and radically and rapidly changes the payoffs of participants. This leads to specific policy recommendations, which we discuss in Section 5.2.

Can we eradicate clientelism? In the final section of this Element, we argue that this is unlikely. Clientelism never completely disappears. Instead, it evolves. As politics becomes more routinized, the importance of clientel-ism decreases but even in developed democracies we still see remnants of it in aspects of how electoral campaigns are run and laws are made. We provide some potential explanations for the different developmental phases of clien-telism. We also discuss specific avenues for future research provided by our perspective.

Before turning to the rest of this Element, we clarify the scope conditions of the analysis. We confine attention in this Element to democratic settings, because clientelism is a key way for politicians to connect with citizens in competitive efforts to gain votes. Nondemocratic settings may feature phenom-ena that resemble clientelism, but since electoral competition is truncated in nondemocratic political systems, clientelism is by definition not part of a com-petitive effort to gain votes; instead, where it appears, politicians use it for other ends. In our definition of democracy, we include regimes that are often labeled "electoral authoritarian," meaning regimes that feature electoral competition even without alternation of executive office. We do not enter into a discussion of whether these regimes should be classed as democratic or authoritarian or if one should prefer a dichotomous definition.[2] Our interest here is in any political system where national-level elected officials undertake activities appealing to citizens in attempts at reelection. In this Element, we thus rely on an expansive and somewhat loose definition of "democracy" in order to include hybrid regimes in our consideration of political systems whose leaders are elected and are obliged to demonstrate responsiveness to voters. Finally, almost all the recent empirical research that we examine reports results from micro-level research within countries in Africa, Latin America, and South Asia. Thus, these areas represent the regional foci of the literature we review.

2 Dimensions of Clientelism

We define clientelism as *the discretionary use by politicians of resources for electoral purposes.*

This definition exhibits several key features. These include *discretion* in the allocation of *resources* (goods or services), the accompanying potential *excludability* of recipients, the *public* nature of the political actor, and the electoral *goal* of the political actor. The definition is silent on the type of resources involved. It encompasses elected and unelected political actors at multiple possible levels in the political system. It omits any notion of exchange, conditionality, or contingency. We discuss these various aspects of our definition before turning to possible conceptual refinements.

2.1 Our Definition Discussed

2.1.1 Key Components

Clientelism does not exist without discretion. Discretion makes voters dependent on politicians. Without discretion, voters either automatically get help from the state – in the form of entitlements, for instance – or get nothing. Of course, the dependency of voters (clients) on politicians (patrons) is never absolute in the modern world; in this regard, modern clientelism is quite different from its premodern counterpart, where the life of the peasant might literally lie in the hands of the landlord. In the modern world, voters are often able to access government services through multiple channels and, conversely, they may receive goods they do not particularly need or value (such as trivial campaign

---

[2] A minimalist definition distinguishes regime type on the basis of a small number of objective characteristics, including whether multiparty elections for executive and legislative offices are held and whether alternation in executive office occurs (Przeworski et al., 2000). Dichotomous definitions do not admit hybrid regimes (Levitsky & Way, 2010), which empirically are a growing phenomenon. However, dichotomous definitions are conceptually parsimonious and exhibit high inter-coder reliability.

paraphernalia) from a politician. Voters are also not powerless even when they are thrust into the role of clients. They can potentially punish their elected representative at the ballot box or organize collectively to extract resources from politicians. But it is difficult for citizens to activate collective responses. And because politicians can retract favors or allocate their discretionary disbursements to others, the relationship between representative and voter is not one of equals.[3] In clientelism, even when voters can shop among contending patrons, as some studies report (Auerbach & Thachil, 2018), political actors retain myriad resources that average voters lack. Patrons, at whatever level, retain advantages when dealing with clients.

There are many types of resources that political actors control and voters do not. Some politicians have access to constituency development funds or other types of funds allocated to the electoral area that lie under his discretion. Almost by definition, a politician can make use of a network of agents (brokers or even government employees) acting on his behalf. Politicians can draw on private or family wealth. They can (perhaps illegitimately) reallocate parts of the state or local budget. They can choose how to allocate their time. Politicians have direct access to other government officials, access that ordinary citizens do not have. In addition, politicians can employ their political stature or social capital to pressure other administrative agents. All of these activities can be deployed in the context of clientelism.

Given discretion, resources are distributed to some voters but not others; that is, some are excluded. No one is entitled to a specific disbursement, nor is there any enforcement agency that can be called upon if a claimant does not receive what he contends is his due. Excludability is part of what renders voters dependent on the politician; because resources are disbursed at the discretion of the politician, the politician can decide that previous recipients no longer receive any. The resources that are disbursed are thus by their nature scarce or they would not provide clientelistic leverage.[4]

Our definition is silent on the beneficiaries of clientelism. We believe that either individuals and groups may be on the receiving end. Politicians may offer gifts or services to particular voters. Or officeholders may offer local public or club goods, such as schools or access to the electricity grid. Politicians may help specific groups or special interests with targeted subsidies. If these goods or services are disbursed via discretion with an electoral goal in mind, they all fall under the definition of clientelism that we propose.

---

[3] We do not distinguish between favors provided directly by candidates from those provided by their agents (brokers). We refer to both types of actors as "politicians."

[4] An alternative formulation is to consider clientelism an outgrowth of the scarcity of state resources and underdevelopment, as suggested by Scott (1972).

Finally, we advance that resources are not disbursed thanks simply to the beneficence of politicians. Instead, they are used with a clear goal in mind: that of improving the politician's electoral fortunes. Clientelism, in our view, is part of an electoral strategy; that is, it is one technique political aspirants use to attract voters (either for their own benefit, in the case of office-seeking politicians, or for the benefit of their faction or group, in the case of the operatives of politicians). Indeed, in its simplest form, clientelism is naked vote buying: the exchange of money or private goods for a vote. More subtly, clientelism may be a defensive strategy, put into operation when politicians fear losing votes if they do not intervene to deliver resources to some voters. It may alternatively be a way to secure new votes or the votes of new voters or a way to suppress turnout. It may improve the lives of voters or portend potential ruin. Regardless of all these possible differences, we define clientelism as undertaken with the goal of gaining (or staying in) office. We do not exclude the fact that politicians may want to win elections to enrich themselves, but this motive is not relevant to clientelism per se. Many politicians seek personal enrichment whether they use clientelist electoral techniques or are exclusively committed to programmatic politics. Indeed, why politicians want to win elections may be highly variable: for personal gain, for social status, to fulfill policy objectives. Clientelism consists of the discretionary disbursements that politicians undertake to win office, regardless of why they seek office or how they behave on other dimensions if elected.

Invoking Harold Lasswell's definition of politics – who gets what, when, and how (Lasswell, 1936) – clientelism in our perspective is about the *how*: it is politics operating via discretion.[5] Whether individuals or groups (the *who*) obtain favors is not consequential to our definition. Whether clientelism is provided before elections or later (the *when*) is of less interest, though timing distinctions can be useful in thinking about types of clientelism, as our distinction between campaign and welfare clientelism suggests. Whether the goods are private or public – or drawn from public funds or private resources – is not directly relevant to our definition.

2.1.2 Comparison with Other Definitions

Having presented our definition of clientelism, let us now contrast it with alternatives. This exercise will also prove useful when we discuss interpretations of different forms of clientelism in Section 3 of this Element.

---

[5] Distributive politics, by contrast, involves the *what*, as pointed out in Golden and Min (2013, p. 74). We also thank Stephane Wolton for reminding us of the connection between clientelism and Harold Laswell's definition of politics.

Well before political scientists, anthropologists and historians were interested in clientelism. Their studies depicted rural landlord-peasant relations as personalistic, reciprocal, hierarchical dyads, in which landlords both exploited and protected peasants and peasants acknowledged and deferred to the power and authority of the landlord (Silverman, 1965; Wolf, 1966). These settings were pre-political, in the sense that patronage and clientelism structured personal and employment relationships – and in fact, "clients" at that time were excluded from formal political participation. The understanding of clientelism evolved with the development of universal suffrage and modern political institutions even in less developed and still largely rural societies (Schmidte et al., 1977; Weingrod, 1968). As governments gradually took on the role of providing basic security and welfare to citizens, political parties and politicians emerged as crucial intermediaries for citizens in accessing welfare and security. The term "clientelism" thus extended to cover the interactions between political organizations and citizens in large-scale modernizing settings, where automatic access to welfare and security was unavailable and discretion a natural part of the political landscape. The typical story that was told was of new mass parties that disbursed goods and services to poor voters in exchange for electoral support; canonical examples included the Italian Christian Democratic Party in large southern cities (Chubb, 1982) and the Indian Congress Party (Brass, 1965).

It is still common for political scientists to conceive of clientelism as an exchange, in which a politician provide goods or services to voters and voters, in return, provide electoral support to the politician. The understanding of clientelism as a conditional or contingent exchange is a central feature of much literature on the topic. Both Hicken (2011, fig. 1, p. 296) and Stokes et al. (2013, fig. 1.1, p. 7) define clientelism as *discretionary targeted* benefits that are *contingent* on voters' support, although Stokes et al. prefer the term "nonprogrammatic policies" to discretionary spending.

We believe insistence on contingency to be unnecessarily restrictive. We are hardly the first to make this argument. As Hicken and Nathan (2020, p. 4) notes, "common usage of the word clientelism now extends significantly beyond the concept's standard definition," and some studies have accordingly removed the contingency component entirely. Kramon (2018), like Gans-Morse et al. (2014), defines campaign clientelism simply as the allocation of material benefits to voters during elections. Diaz-Cayeros et al. (2016, fig. 1.1, p. 8) see clientelism as the discretionary allocation of private goods.

Our definition builds directly on the perspective that eliminates any notion of contingency; we stress instead a single critical element of clientelism: its discretionary nature. We extend the emphasis on discretion by removing any specific temporal constraint; that is, clientelism does not have to occur during election campaigns but may also occur between them. Finally, we remove any restriction on the types of goods allocated or resources employed: clientelism does not necessarily involve private (as opposed to public) goods. Our definition is close in spirit to Hicken and Nathan's (2020) hands-off approach: "[T]aking scholars at their word and considering together all of the nonprogrammatic strategies they choose to label as clientelism" (p. 4). Unlike this view, however, we do not think that all nonprogrammatic strategies are clientelistic. Instead, we limit our definition to cover activities with clear electoral objectives. Finally, we do not think that clientelism is restricted to nonprogrammatic distributions; it can also pervert programmatic policy allocations. We return to this last point when we distinguish legal from illegal clientelism.

Our perspective on clientelism is thus that it is a broad phenomenon. Nonetheless, we do not think scholars should use the term "clientelism" as a default or catchall term. To clarify this, we now compare our definition of clientelism with the concepts of distributive politics and corruption.

2.1.3 Clientelism, Distributive Politics, and Corruption

We first distinguish clientelism from distributive politics. Golden and Min (2013, p. 74) define distributive policies as those that "involve taxes and transfers, and in particular the decisions about allocations of government goods and services to identifiable localities or groups." Distributive policies can thus be programmatic. Taxes can be imposed according to clear rules, and indeed often are. Transfers can be made according to established and publicized formulas. Transfers that occur via earmarks, as in the United States, are, according to our definition, not clientelistic because they require congressional approval and thus do not fall under the discretion of single politicians. Like clientelism, earmarks have clear electoral ends and benefit-specific localities, but not every electorally oriented policy is clientelistic. Nor is discretion the modus operandi of all distributive policies.

Some distributive policies, however, are dependent on the decisions of single officeholders. Some of what are referred to as "pork-barrel" policies provide an example; these include the discretionary allocation of club goods to specific localities. The allocation of a representative's constituency development fund – funds available in many developing countries around the world – is one way this occurs because, by definition, the representative has discretion over the funds allocated to his district. Even in developed democracies, politicians may have discretion over how to allocate block grants that come to their electoral districts.

Does this make clientelism a subset of distributive politics? Or is clientelism simply distributive policies over which politicians have discretion? We suggest not. Distributive policies are by definition about public resources, whereas nothing prevents politicians using their own private income or donors' contributions to finance clientelism. Distributive policies target groups and localities, whereas clientelism may be directed at individuals. Although the two concepts partially overlap, one does not encompass the other and they are not identical.

Clientelism also differs from corruption, whether defined as "acts in which the power of public office is used for personal gain in a manner that contravenes the rules of the game" (Jain, 2001, p. 73) or more simply as "the misuse of public resources and power for private gains" (Sequeira, 2012, p. 146). Both definitions share the view that corruption involves the abuse of public office and note, by implication, that such abuse often involves illegality. Clientelism, by contrast, may be employed by a private individual who seeks public office. Furthermore, our understanding of clientelism does not imply that it is necessarily illegal, that it contravenes the "rules of the game," or even that it is discordant with social norms. Some clientelistic activities are corrupt – for instance, granting public benefits in exchange for a bribe or using cash to buy votes. But others are not, instead leveraging the legitimate discretion of a public official. And clientelism may be normatively acceptable to voters.

Our relatively broad understanding of clientelism has, we believe, several advantages over other definitions; in particular, it allows us to identify clientelistic practices across all levels of economic development. As we discuss at greater length in the concluding section in this Element, we identify variants of clientelism even in the world's economically most developed nations. The broad definition that we propose captures these as well as the more well-studied clientelist activities in less developed settings.

The definition we propose is not likely to be uncontroversial. To illustrate, consider the following situation. A politician directs discretionary transfers under his control to improve health outcomes in a poor village. Is this clientelism? For some, the answer would be that it is not, on the grounds that health transfers are welfare-improving, recipients potentially include the entire community, and the politician's access to the funds was legitimate and rule-abiding. From our perspective, these transfers would be classed as clientelistic if an alternative allocation would have been more equitable, perhaps involving transfers to other villages where the politician's political standing was different, and assuming the inequitable feature of the allocation was deliberately orchestrated for electoral purposes.[6] Consider, similarly, the use of discretionary funds to provide relief to an area affected by a natural disaster, such as an earthquake or flood. For us, whether these distributions are clientelistic hinges on whether there are other, more equitable (but electorally less opportune) distributions that the politician could have made had he not taken the potential electoral returns into consideration. Thus, we bracket clientelism by the *goal* of the key actor: clientelism is defined by its electoral objectives. Sometimes discretionary disbursements are identical to the most equitable and the electorally most opportune. In these cases, we may be hard-pressed to claim an allocation was clientelist. But often, there is a difference, and this difference is what allows us to identify clientelistic practices empirically.

2.2 Categories of Clientelism

Clientelism, as we have defined it, is distinct from distributive politics and corruption; it is identified by its discretionary nature and its political goal. But not all clientelism is the same. We now provide some refinements within our definition. We distinguish legal from illegal clientelism, individual from collective clientelism, public from private clientelism, and campaign from welfare clientelism.

2.2.1 Legal and Illegal Clientelism

One direct implication of our definition is that clientelism is not necessarily illegal. When officeholders allocate constituency development funds, for instance, or other discretionary funds they may control, they may do so in perfectly legal ways. Observers may object that the funds do not reach those who need them most or ought to receive them, but these are questions of welfare, not legality. When political representatives meet with voters and provide services, such as facilitating paperwork requests, helping citizens get back on the ration list, or helping the needy access a government medical facility, typically these activities are perfectly legal even if recipients are selected on a partisan or other electorally relevant basis.

There are, of course, occasions when politicians engage in clientelism and, in so doing, break the law. There are two main ways this can happen. First, a representative may have legal access to some government resource, including funds, but may use it in an illegal way. Second, a politician may use discretion when none is legally accorded.

---

[6] We set aside issues of measurement here. We grant that obtaining clear and unequivocal measures of these features is difficult, but that does not mean they cannot be shown to be at work.

A well-known example of the first form of illegal clientelism includes vote buying, which is illegal in all but six countries (Ohman, 2012). A parallel illegal use of government funds is turnout buying, which consists of paying voters to go to the polls (Nichter, 2008). In some countries, even transporting voters to the polling place is illegal; where it is not – as in the United States – it is illegal to reimburse them for the associated costs. These are all activities that, depending on the statutes in place, may constitute illegal clientelism. The direct exchange of development funds for campaign contributions would in most cases be another example of illegal clientelism. In general, all illegal forms of quid pro quo belong in this category.

The second form of illegal clientelism corresponds to a perversion of programmatic policies or practices. Colonnelli et al. (2020) describe how mayors in Brazil reward their political supporters with jobs in the government bureaucracy even when the activists lack the necessary job requirements. By doing this, officeholders are reintroducing patronage into a merit-based civil service system, a practice long ago perfected by mayors of large cities in the United States (Key, 1935). Political representatives can also pressure bureaucrats or decide themselves to grant benefits to recipients who would otherwise not be entitled to them, thereby violating the law. Programmatic policies, with their clear and publicized rules, are not enough to eliminate clientelism, although they clearly restrict its use.

2.2.2 Individual and Collective Clientelism

Clientelism is often viewed as targeting individual citizens. Indeed, many well-known clientelist activities consist of trivial gifts – T-shirts, mugs, pens – that publicly identify the political candidate a voter supports, thereby encouraging the voter to cast a ballot for the candidate. Clientelism can also take the form of delivering services to individuals in need. From help with a paperwork request or land titling to financing a funeral, many interactions between clients (citizens) and patrons (politicians or their agents) take place on the most microscopic scale.

Nonetheless, individual interactions do not encompass the full extent of clientelism. Clientelism may also involve the allocation of collective goods – disbursements to a group of voters, an entire village, or a specific industry. Min and Golden (2014) offer the example of the politicized use of electricity line losses – in the context of the northern Indian state under study, this means unbilled electricity distribution to entire rural communities that otherwise would lack electricity – in the preelectoral period. In a similar vein, Khemani (2004) documents election-year targeting of tax breaks for special interests – examples provided include those involved in the production of spirits and narcotics – using data from fourteen Indian states over a thirty-year period. The study interprets these preelection tax breaks as aimed at "campaign finance or mobilization of political support through local influence" (p. 129), an evaluation that accords well with our definition of clientelism. Collective clientelism also takes the form of distributing local public goods, such as schools, roads, sanitation projects, or the construction of new market places. Although national governments make broad commitments to providing such goods, actual implementation may be left to the discretion of subnational levels of government, including provincial or state governments as well as local levels.

2.2.3 Private and Public Clientelism

We might also differentiate private and public clientelism based on the resources employed. We label clientelism "private" when politicians make use of private resources, be it their own or their donors'. When instead politicians employ government resources, we label clientelism "public."

One reason we introduce the term "private" clientelism is to remind readers that candidates for public office – and not only officeholders – engage in clientelistic practices. They may disburse privately financed gifts, favors, or treats to voters in efforts to convince them that the candidate would make a helpful representative. Indeed, scholars in settings known for high levels of clientelism often remark that only the wealthy can afford to run for office precisely because of the weight of campaign expenses, including handouts to voters.

The distinction between public and private clientelism is more difficult to make when it comes to an officeholder's time. Representatives allocate many hours to receiving constituents and listening to their complaints (Berenschot, 2010; Bussell, 2019). As a rule of thumb, we might say that any meeting held at an official, regular time – what the British call surgeries by Members of Parliament – falls under the category of public clientelism. Any meeting held at other times or on an ad hoc basis – while traveling in the constituency on personal errands for example – would be considered private clientelism. But for most purposes, this distinction is of less importance than the provenance of a politician's funds.

2.2.4 Campaign and Welfare Clientelism

We end this section with one last distinction, which we return to again in the next section. Like other scholars (e.g., Nichter, 2018), we see the literature on clientelism as attending to two distinct phenomena: what is depicted as politicians' actions to gain votes on the campaign trail, on the one hand, and what is depicted as the quotidian nonprogrammatic interactions of politicians and citizens to solve problems and provide services in low-capacity state settings, on the other. The literature often labels the first "electoral" clientelism, but since all clientelism is meant to improve a politician's electoral returns, we prefer the term "campaign" clientelism. For the second, these interactions have been labeled "relational" clientelism, although we prefer "welfare" clientelism because we think the latter term conveys more precise content. The two are theoretically and empirically distinguishable on the basis of *when* in the electoral cycle they occur.

We define campaign clientelism using a common denominator evident in many other studies: handouts by politicians in the period prior to an election. In the contemporary political science literature, campaign clientelism is far and away the best studied type of clientelism. It forms the heart of the work by Stokes et al. (2013), the most-cited book on the topic in the decade of scholarship that we review. Handouts that occur as part of campaign clientelism are not gifts – in the sense of expecting nothing in return – but rather are provided by politicians with the aim of improving their electoral fortunes. They lie entirely within the discretion of the politician.

Election handouts potentially involve the distribution of individual goods or, more broadly, timing public expenditures in relation to the election cycle. For instance, Sáez and Sinha (2010) identify election timing as a salient factor in public expenditures in India over a two-decade period. Similarly, Akhmedov and Zhuravskaya (2004) documents electoral cycles in public spending aimed at Russian voters. These studies corroborate the literature on political business cycles (Canes-Wrone & Park, 2012; Kramer, 1971; Tufte, 1978), which holds that politicians manipulate their budgets to enlarge spending in the run-up to elections in order to woo voters. Whether such manipulations qualify as clientelism depends, according to our definition, mainly on whether budget manipulations take place via discretionary decisions on the part of individual politicians or whether instead they occur via legislation enacted collectively by elected officials. We do not consider legislative enactments voted on collectively in the representative chamber as clientelism because such enactments lack the defining discretionary feature of our definition. However, to the extent that public spending in the preelectoral period takes place via a series of discretionary disbursements by individual politicians, it qualifies as clientelism. Of course, aggregate spending outcomes do not themselves provide the information necessary to know whether disbursements were clientelistic; this requires instead understanding how the decisions were made and by whom.

Clientelism does not merely arise before an election only to disappear when polling stations close. Scholars have also looked at ongoing clientelistic relations between politicians and constituents. This dimension of clientelism involves efforts by politicians to respond to constituent requests to secure access to or benefits from the state. These interactions are sometimes unflatteringly depicted as the outcome of the aggressively frequent visits by politicians to their constituencies in order to cultivate relations of dependency with voters. Others, however, contend that these ongoing interactions emerge at the active request of voters (Bussell, 2019; Kramon, 2018; Kruks-Wisner, 2018). The latter view highlights that clientelism may reciprocally benefit both politicians and voters, a point on which we expand in Section 5 of this Element.

Welfare clientelism, which can again be collective or individual, occurs when politicians operate in environments where voters are economically vulnerable and subject to risk, an understanding similar to that of Nichter (2018). The types of services provided may take different forms. We briefly summarize them here, using a slightly amended classification adapted from Berenschot (2010).

We divide welfare clientelism into three categories: (1) requests for information about the operations of government or for assistance accessing government services to which the individual or community is entitled (an identity card, a ration booklet, duplication of missing land records, etc.); (2) requests for discretionary goods or services to which the individual or community is not necessarily entitled but which are potentially available (an electricity connection, a business license, street lights, etc.); and (3) requests for discretionary goods or services to which the individual or community is not entitled and access to which cannot legally be given (enrollment in a jobs program when the individual does not qualify, the illegal diversion of development funds to a community that does not meet requisite criteria, etc.). The literature labels the first "constituency service," the second "clientelism," and the third "corruption." All, however, are problems voters in low-income settings need solved by politicians. This is illustrated in a study based on intensive field research that included shadowing a local Indian politician for more than a year (Berenschot, 2010). As long as politicians employ discretionary means to help their constituents (individually or as a group) in the hope of cultivating votes, all activities fit our definition of clientelism.

Welfare clientelism is, thus, distinguished from campaign clientelism on the basis of when it arises. Campaign clientelism is restricted in time to the electoral period; welfare clientelism, by contrast, occurs on an ongoing basis. Campaign clientelism typically consists of gifts or favors; welfare clientelism is a way to resolve problems or to respond to specific needs arising during a politician's term. In some cases, the two are difficult to distinguish. When voters organize themselves, they may negotiate as a bloc with politicians for infrastructure projects (Chandra, 2004, 2007; Mohmand, 2019; Srinivas, 1955). Bloc leaders essentially take bids from contenders for public office, and then instruct their members how to vote on the basis of whichever bid is accepted. In this process, communities extract costly promises from politicians, who themselves have strong electoral incentives to fulfill them, a process described in Mohmand (2019). This process blurs the distinction between campaign and welfare clientelism because public goods are provided during the representative's term based on promises that were made during the electoral campaign. As a result, some disbursements may not neatly sort into one of the two categories that we advance.

With existing definitions and our own in mind, we now turn to various interpretations of clientelism found in the literature.

3 Interpretations of Clientelism in Existing Literature

In the last decade, the topic of clientelism has elicited a rich and vigorous debate. Perhaps surprisingly, the literature has evolved coherently, in the sense that scholars have built on previous work to solve open questions, each study scaffolding the next. To showcase the theoretical evolution of the literature, we present a (short and simplified) history of studies on campaign clientelism. We then turn to the newer interest in welfare clientelism. We conclude this section with a discussion of whether campaign and welfare clientelism are substitutes or complements.

3.1 Interpretations of Campaign Clientelism

For many years, stemming at least from Cox and Kousser (1981), political science has viewed campaign clientelism as a form of vote buying. This economic interpretation of the relations between voters and politicians appears natural. After all, if politicians provide cash or other goods to voters – whiskey, food, clothing – it must be that the former expect something in return. And this "something" has to be what politicians value most: votes. This interpretation is not only intuitively plausible but grounded in the historical record. In the United Kingdom in the nineteenth century, candidates' agents were tasked with "recruiting" voters and were given special funds for this purpose (Kam, 2017). In the United States, urban political machines organized voters' processions to the poll, a phenomenon vividly depicted in Martin Scorsese's *Gangs of New York* and studied in Trounstine (2008).

Yet for all its intuitive appeal, this interpretation quickly runs into trouble. First, the theory of vote buying predicts that politicians should target swing voters, or those who have yet to be persuaded in their vote choice, rather than core supporters, who will vote for a party regardless (see Stokes [2005], who draws on Dixit and Londregan [1996]). After all, there is no reason to "buy" votes from people who are sure bets to begin with. But as scholarly interest in the theory of campaign-clientelism-as-vote-buying grew, researchers uncovered facts at odds with this supposition. Empirical research shows that a substantial proportion of politicians' funds which are devoted to campaign clientelism appears to be directed at core supporters (for a discussion see Stokes et al., 2013). This makes clientelism conceptually problematic: why would politicians undertake activities that appear to consist of "vote buying" for votes they already know they will receive? In addition, vote buying presents a fundamental conceptual paradox because of the temporal and informational asymmetries that underlie it. A candidate hands out something today expecting the voter to cast a ballot for him in the (more or less) near future. But because the vote is secret, there is no way to verify that the voter holds up her end of the bargain.[7] In the contemporary world, voters can simply pocket any gifts they are offered and vote as they wish, as others have noted (Hicken & Nathan, 2020; Schaffer, 2007). The 2021 election in Zambia serves as a case in point. Despite the fact that paraphernalia distributed by the incumbent president, Edgar Lungu, dominated the streets of the capital, the opposition candidate, Hakainde Hichilema, won the election in a landslide. To be left in peace during the run-up to the vote, some Zambians adopted what was locally called the "watermelon strategy," after the identifying colors of the two candidates. Voters wore green – the color of the president – but planned to vote red – the color of the opposition.[8] The inability to ensure that voters fulfill their promises makes vote buying problematic for politicians. This is confirmed by historical data from the United Kingdom, which show that the price of a vote fell dramatically following the 1872 introduction of the secret ballot, from £5 to a mere 5 shillings (Seymour, 1915). The secret ballot rendered vote buying logistically infeasible. Once politicians could not directly observe the vote, the exchange was no longer enforceable, and the value of a vote dropped dramatically.

In standard Kuhnian fashion, faced with unexpected and discordant facts, scholars first thought to amend the theory of vote buying. This was accomplished primarily by introducing brokers into the campaign clientelism mix (Stokes et al., 2013).[9] Brokers play a double role in the amended framework.

---

[7] Even with public ballots — which are currently used in only two countries in the world anyway (Przeworski, 2015, p. 97) — vote buying is illegal, meaning there is no legitimate enforcement mechanism to hold voters accountable if they renege on their promises. As we have already noted, almost all countries prohibit vote buying.

[8] See www.lemonde.fr/afrique/article/2021/08/10/election-presidentielle-en-zambie-confrontee-a-une-montagne-de-dettes_6091052_3212.html.

[9] Scholars have also uncovered subtle ways that politicians buy votes that do not require monitoring. A trivial mechanism is to split the delivery of a clientelistic good into two parts, the second of which is contingent on the politician's victory. A canonical example is a pair of

First, brokers are agents of candidates but also have their own interests (summarized by the goal of minimizing effort). Second, brokers monitor constituents to ensure they go to the polls and vote the right way. But even if we admit an agent specifically tasked with monitoring, how does (s)he achieve it in the context of the secret ballot?

Brokers are said to use local, idiosyncratic, and information-sensitive techniques to successfully circumvent the secret ballot. An oft-cited example includes what is in some places known as the Tasmanian Dodge – it goes by many other names, however – which involves having the voter deposit a ballot already filled out and returning an empty ballot to the person monitoring the vote. Other methods are available when the paper ballot that is used does not correspond to the uniform Australian ballot but instead is color-coded to be partisan-identified, as is still the case in various countries, including Argentina and Bolivia, among others (Reynolds & Steenbergen, 2006), or when direct observation of the voting process is possible due to local idiosyncrasies, such as when brokers require voters to submit a cell phone photo of their ballot. Ballot secrecy is clearly more easily breached when the number of voters at the polling station is very small (Caselli & Falco, in press; Rueda, 2017), because such settings make it is easier to ascertain which individuals are likely to have violated their contracts. Even then, when brokers compare expected and realized tallies they can know only that some voters reneged on their promises. They cannot identify the specific voters. To make things more complicated, brokers often do not control the votes of an entire precinct. There may be uncertainty about how many votes the broker's candidate should actually receive. All of this suggests that monitoring the polls is always imperfect. Even the supposition that brokers know their clients has been questioned. In India, Schneider (2020) shows that brokers are largely unable to guess accurately how the voters they monitor in fact cast their ballots.

Monitoring of polling stations alone is thus insufficient. Because of this, monitoring is complemented by social interactions and expectations. Settings where politicians and their agents have intimate and daily interactions with their constituents facilitate brokers' tasks. In tight social settings, it is more difficult for voters to disguise their vote choice from friends, family and, as

shoes: one shoe is delivered prior to the election but receiving the mate is dependent on the outcome of the election. Another clever example comes from the 2000 Taiwanese presidential election, when the ruling party subsidized betting parlors to offer extremely favorable odds in the event that the party's candidate was elected, thereby providing the prospect of financial gain to those ready to endorse that candidate (reported in Morgan and Várdy [2011, p. 261]). These measures, however, seem to be exceptional rather than the norm, at least according to what it documented in the scholarly literature.

a result, political operatives. Yet it is not clear which types of social environments satisfy these conditions and how widespread they are. Instead, it seems that regardless of the social setting, brokers may manipulate the expectations of voters. This is because of the common belief among voters that their vote is not really secret. Surprisingly, this is the case even in countries where such suspicion seems patently unwarranted. Gerber et al. (2013) report that 20 percent of voters in the United States believe their vote is not secret; proportions rise to between 25 and 35 percent in settings where democratic processes are more recently established and more fragile, such as Argentina (Stokes, 2005), Nicaragua (Gonzalez-Ocantos et al., 2012), and Ghana (Ferree & Long, 2016).[10] Thus, brokers can play off the fact that large numbers of voters believe their votes can be known to others, even when scholars judge this highly improbable.

Given these inaccurate beliefs, we might say that monitoring works because it is believed to be working by the monitored. But that appears to be a fragile basis on which to construct a successful electoral strategy, and particularly one that endures over time. There is little evidence that candidates for office anywhere in the democratic world currently can access the information that would permit them to enforce regular large-scale vote-buying exchanges. Candidates no longer control the weapons that require voters to cast their ballot for a specific candidate or risk extreme measures – including complete destitution – as used to occur prior to the introduction of the secret ballot (for evidence, see Baland & Robinson, 2008; Mares, 2015). Once voters are made aware that no one will know if they vote their conscience, many vote for their preferred candidate (Arias et al., 2019; Blattman et al., 2019; Vasudevan, 2019; Vicente, 2014). Candidates, however, do not appear to change their behavior and desist from offering clientelistic inducements even when voters are reminded that their votes are secret, a point we return to in Section 5.

Although the numbers of voters who think others know how they vote are impressive and somewhat depressing, they should not be over-interpreted. All studies show that in democratic countries, the vast majority of voters know their vote is secret; even in very poor countries, where vote buying is relatively common, most voters are aware that their votes are secret (Kramon, 2018, p. 80). This suggests that vote buying only affects a small proportion of the electorate, rendering it of limited empirical importance and highly dependent on conditions on the ground.

---

[10] In authoritarian regimes that sponsor elections, even higher rates of voters believe their votes are not secret. Ostwald and Riambau (2017) report that in Singapore, somewhere between a third and as much as half the electorate believes the ballot is not secret.

Despite the recent attention they have generated thanks to Stokes et al. (2013), brokers appear inadequate to save the vote-buying interpretation of clientelism. In fact, in a recent review, the whole line of argument has been labeled a "red herring" (Hicken & Nathan, 2020) – in other words, a distraction from the job of providing a valid theoretical understanding of why politicians distribute handouts in preelectoral periods. Theoretical alternatives to brokers have not been long in coming. Some scholars have turned to another, loosely related explanation for vote buying: norms of reciprocity (Finan & Schechter, 2012; Lawson & Greene, 2014). Where politicians can play on norms of reciprocity, they can induce voter loyalty and be more confident that the voter does her part. This naturally raises the question of how norms of reciprocity are sustained and operate over time. If reciprocity were key, interventions that inform voters that their votes are not monitored should find no effect of such information campaigns. Instead, voters should retain their electoral loyalty to the candidate who provided them something, in an effort to reciprocate. Yet, as we have already noted, these campaigns tend to reduce the impact of clientelism (Arias et al., 2019; Blattman et al., 2019; Vasudevan, 2019; Vicente, 2014).[11] Thus, not much is required for voters to have their cake and eat it too – take the goods offered by a candidate and then vote as they prefer. Since information campaigns about ballot secrecy are effective, it seems norms of reciprocity are inadequate for sustaining large-scale and ongoing vote buying.

Unable to resolve the monitoring problem, scholars invoked an alternative interpretation: campaign clientelism does not buy votes at all but instead buys turnout. This interpretation aligns with evidence that brokers have multiple ways to encourage turnout and that parties monitor them on their success in this regard (e.g., Larreguy et al., 2020; Nichter, 2008; Szwarcberg, 2015). Some debate exists in the literature about where turnout buying is most likely to occur. Although it is intuitive that brokers facilitate turnout of strong supporters, inducing loyalists to go to the polls (Nichter, 2008), some have theorized that a more efficient strategy would be to aim resources at relatively indifferent voters in opposition strongholds (Casas, 2018). This, however, may be operationally difficult to organize, precisely because of the difficulties of identifying and targeting floating voters in another politician's stronghold. Perhaps it is easier for parties and candidates to engage in negative turnout buying: rather than

---

[11] While there is a lively debate about the effectiveness of providing information to voters for improving political accountability in general (Bhandari et al., in press; Dunning et al., 2019), information campaigns appear relatively successful at breaking ties between voters and candidates that involve vote buying.

induce voters to go to the polls, brokers can "encourage" supporters of other candidates to stay home (Cox & Kousser, 1981; Morgan & Várdy, 2012).

Although empirical issues of targeting remain open, when it was first advanced, the turnout-theory of clientelism seemed a plausible theoretical solution to the monitoring problem of campaign clientelism. However, recent scholarship has uncovered new evidence that casts doubt on the idea that the main task of brokers is to mobilize turnout. Studies document that in some places, brokers do not mobilize voters at all but instead sell preexisting blocs of votes – what are called "vote banks" (Chandra, 2004; Holland & Palmer-Rubin, 2015; Mohmand, 2019; Srinivas, 1955) – to the highest bidder. Along similar lines, Brierley and Nathan (2021) studied brokers in Ghana and show that, contrary to what either vote- or turnout-buying theories predict, parties prefer brokers who are well connected to elites rather than to constituents. Brierley and Nathan (2022) further document that most brokers are paid in periods between elections and only a few are rewarded for their performance during the campaign. The latter suggests that brokers are tools for welfare rather than campaign clientelism, a point we return to below.

Even as scholars debate whether empirical evidence validates theories of vote or turnout buying, a deeper and more fundamental paradigm shift has been under way. Recent studies reconceptualize preelectoral handouts as a signaling game (Kramon, 2018; Muñoz, 2018). This view maintains that the distribution of goods in the preelectoral period is meant to signal the strength of the politician rather than constituting half of an exchange relationship.

Evidence in support of the signaling theory begins with the observation that in many contexts, politicians indiscriminately distribute small "gifts" to voters. Often, no attempt is made to identify the partisan leanings of the recipient before distributing the gift and, similarly, no attempt is made to follow up in order to ascertain whether the recipient delivered her vote in exchange. This suggests that the intention of the distribution cannot be to buy votes and indeed, that the distribution of benefits is not one side of an exchange at all.

The informational-signaling argument holds particular appeal where political parties are weak and lack the on-the-ground manpower and technologies required to enforce vote-buying exchanges in the first place (Muñoz, 2018). In these contexts, it is not difficult to imagine that politicians provide handouts in order to induce voters to attend campaign rallies, to adorn themselves in branded paraphernalia, or to otherwise contribute to the impression that a candidate is politically viable. But there is no specific reason why information signaling with campaign clientelism may not also be in play in settings with more developed parties. During their heyday, the Italian Christian Democrats – a highly developed and finely articulated political party if there ever was one – are reported to have driven trucks of pasta into poor neighborhoods in Palermo, accompanied by "thousands of ballot facsimiles with the candidate's name and number" (Chubb, 1982, p. 170).

Although the informational approach obviates the monitoring conundrum, important questions remain unanswered. For example, the literature has not yet explored sufficiently whether the targets of candidates' signals are core or swing voters, and whether and under what conditions the goal of signaling is to persuade undecided citizens to vote for the candidate, to motivate supporters to turn out, or perhaps both. There is also debate regarding the exact nature of the signal sent by politicians. Kramon (2018) sees gift-giving as a way to show that the candidate is aware of constituents' needs. Muñoz (2018) argues that it demonstrates the candidate has the financial prowess to wage an effective electoral campaign and hence win the seat. Aspinall and Berenschot (2019) hold that handouts are a sign that if elected, a candidate will continue to direct resources to his constituents. We await additional theoretical and empirical research to discriminate among or amalgamate these various possibilities. In addition, as we stress in Section 5, the signaling theory would benefit from explicit formalization and linkage to the Grossman and Helpman (2001) theoretical framework.

The literature on campaign clientelism has developed in a piecemeal and spontaneous fashion rather than having been coordinated centrally in an effort to build cross-site knowledge (cf. Dunning et al., 2019). Nonetheless, our view is that it has progressed in a way that contributes to knowledge. We agree with Hicken and Nathan (2020) that after a decade's worth of research, there is ample evidence that clientelism exists and operates without having to invoke any assumption of contingency or investments in monitoring. Along with a growing number of other scholars, we contend it is time to lay to rest the contingency assumption in our understanding of clientelism. This, we believe, is one element that demonstrates the rapid progress that the debate on campaign clientelism has brought with it: in less than a decade, working almost entirely independently, scores of researchers have thoroughly delimited, delineated, and countered the theory that campaign clientelism constitutes a contingent exchange implemented on one side by brokers. At least two amendments have been introduced – the reciprocity theory and the theory of turnout buying – followed by an alternative theory focusing on information. Intellectual progress appears cumulative in the sense that later works correct, refine, and displace earlier studies. The topic has been surprisingly fruitful in improving understanding and gradually building intellectual consensus.

3.2 Interpretations of Welfare Clientelism

We turn now to the second type of clientelism investigated by recent literature: welfare clientelism, or the discretionary provision of goods and services between elections. The relevant body of scholarship is smaller than that regarding campaign clientelism and perhaps less visible; the phenomenon does not figure at all, for instance, in the recent review by Hicken and Nathan (2020). As with campaign clientelism, welfare clientelism has also been seen through the prism of contingent exchange. In this vein, it is interpreted as a stick that politicians use to encourage voters to vote for them. Some have contended that voters who do not support the incumbent are barred from access to the vital services provided by his office between elections. Brokers who sniff out a constituent who voted for the opposition will simply refuse to provide help to that person (Stokes et al., 2013).

Intuitively, there seems little doubt that partisan supporters should be the main beneficiaries of welfare clientelism, since targeting them for assistance helps keep supporters politically loyal. Not surprisingly, studies thus document consistent partisan favoritism in how politicians (and other public officials) respond to requests from individual voters for help with matters of health and jobs (for instance, Nichter [2018, ch. 3]). Copartisans request help more frequently than voters not affiliated with their representative's political party, and are more likely to receive it upon asking. A trivial, but disconcerting, illustration involves accessing public medical assistance: a declared copartisan might get an indispensable root canal from a public dentist, whereas a noncopartisan is forced to undergo an extraction instead (Nichter, 2018, p. 121).

In its most extreme form, welfare clientelism takes the form of distributing patronage jobs.[12] A job is a highly targeted way to create a deeply committed loyalist. Patronage jobs align the incentives of the voter with those of the politician such that the voter has his own interest in the continued electoral success of the politician (Mares & Young, 2018; Robinson & Verdier, 2013). But patronage opportunities are limited. The bureaucracy cannot be expanded infinitely – or even sufficiently to accommodate all needy constituents. Hence, patronage jobs, like other forms of clientelism, may well serve as gifts to particularly useful and influential supporters or brokers, those who can carry with them large numbers of additional votes (Cruz, 2019; Schaffer & Baker, 2015) – especially if they are low-skill and hence cheaper to employ (Calvo & Murillo, 2004).

---

[12] Some observers class patronage jobs under campaign clientelism. But because jobs are long-lasting, we incorporate them into welfare clientelism.

Political supporters may well be the main beneficiaries of welfare clientelism, but they are not the sole recipients of politicians' help. Multiple studies document that politicians often provide services to noncopartisans (Bussell, 2019; Nichter, 2018; Thachil, 2014). Even the analysis in Stokes et al. (2013) shows that half of the clients helped by Argentine brokers are not partisan sympathizers (fig. 4.6, p. 114).

What explains this behavior? That is, why would politicians in clientelist settings provide discretionary help to people who did not vote for them? We conjecture that in less developed settings, key variables include the sheer number and nature of requests, which are more frequent and more varied where economic risk is greater and state capacity lower, and the difficulty in monitoring the allegiance of the petitioners, a theme we have already encountered above. In wealthy countries, the underpinnings of impartial assistance to constituents are different; there, blatant partisanship in constituency service would be revealed publicly – by the press, for instance – and violate norms. In less developed democracies, norms of impartiality in the provision of government services are weaker. And because state services are inadequate or ineffectively delivered, so many voters turn to politicians for assistance that it is difficult for them to filter requests on the basis of partisan affiliation or personal loyalty. Moreover, even when it is possible to screen out copartisans from opponents or nonsupporters, it may not be politically prudent to turn them away. Political reputation may turn on the ability to get things done, whether for one's existing supporters or for others.

How does welfare clientelism operate on the ground? Scholars commonly report that in less developed democracies, legislators visit their home constituencies on a weekly basis, where they spend the day receiving streams of visitors who make highly specific requests for urgent material help. A survey of Ghanian Members of Parliament reports that they receive 10–20 constituents a day when in their home constituencies (Lindberg, 2003, p. 129); field work in three states in India estimates that state legislators receive an average of 21 constituents a day (Bussell, 2019, p. 55). In Pakistan, older research reports that politicians receive anywhere from 20 to more than 100 supplicants over the course of a day (Wilder, 1999, p. 199). Individuals approach their elected representatives directly to request assistance for all manner of problems – problems that stem from poverty and a lack of entitlements to government services as well as problems that stem from the poor operation of the state itself. Thus, welfare clientelism is sustained by the absence of a welfare state in combination with weak state capacity.

To be effective in delivering constituency and welfare services, officeholders rely on other agents to do their bidding. This is possible via two distinct channels. First, where government offices do not operate with efficiency or impartiality, citizens turn to elected officials to mediate their relations with the bureaucracy (Berenschot, 2010; Golden, 2003). This renders elected officials central figures in the discretionary distribution of the inadequate goods and services provided by government – such as replacing a lost ration card, obtaining urgent hospital admission, or receiving an unemployment payment. The vicious cycle linking bureaucratic inefficiency and political discretion means that bureaucratic responsiveness hinges on a personal request from a political superior. The second route for service delivery is via the representatives' own network of brokers and fixers. Brokers serve as intermediaries between elected officials and citizens for service provision. Based on ethnographic work and a survey of public employees in three Argentinian municipalities, Oliveros (2016) documents that while all municipal employees grant favors, favoritism is particularly pronounced among patronage workers. City employees who are supporters of the mayor are 30 percentage points more likely to provide benefits than others when asked. Other research reports similar findings: Auyero (2000) reports that in Argentina, "[brokers'] work extends beyond politics and election times. Many serve as centers from which food and medicine are distributed, and brokers can be approached for small favors all year round" (p. 83).

This understanding of how clientelism functions in intra-election periods also explains why some studies report that core districts are favored in receiving assistance from national- or state-level politicians (see Mares and Young [2018], where welfare clientelism is referred to as "preelectoral benefits"). These districts are places where politicians can activate and mobilize the public bureaucracy they control and the party networks they have developed to deliver in response to requests for assistance.

As with individual welfare clientelism, collective welfare clientelism may be more or less one-sided. Much depends on whether voters in communities have found ways to organize collectively to interact with political representatives (Gottlieb & Larreguy, 2020). When they have not, voters are often relatively powerless in their interactions with politicians (Carlitz, 2017). Communities receive little development aid and are left to fend for themselves. This may create a spiral of underdevelopment, where uncoordinated voters and a lack of public funds reinforce each other. But sometimes voters manage to break out of this cycle, especially when they can rely on kinship networks. In some contexts, voters organize and coordinate their requests to politicians and successfully extract development goods. Literature on South Asian villages going back decades reports that caste organizations function this way (Bailey, 1963).

3.3 Campaign and Welfare Clientelism: Substitutes or Complements?

What is the observable relationship between campaign and welfare clientelism? Do politicians who distribute gifts in preelectoral periods also assist voters with welfare needs between elections? Do politicians who provide assistance to individual voters in their constituencies also roll out infrastructure projects to their communities? Or are these various practices undertaken by distinct classes or types of politicians, or directed at different types of voters?

Existing literature does not permit complete answers to these questions. But we can make headway by first examining what various studies report about the frequency of each type of clientelism.

Many studies estimate the frequency of campaign clientelism, the best documented type of clientelism that occurs in the less developed world. In Africa, survey data from the period 2007 to 2011 indicate that around 20 percent of respondents have received something – for instance, "food or a gift or money" – in return for their vote (e.g., Bratton, 2008; Gutiérrez-Romero, 2014). This average, however, masks significant variation, ranging from less than 10 percent in Ghana (Rauschenbach & Katin, 2019) to 40 percent in Kenya and Uganda (Blattman et al., 2019; Kramon, 2018). The overall picture is that campaign clientelism is relatively common in Africa. Literature also finds campaign clientelism to be common in other regions of the world. Stokes (2005, p. 321) reports that according to data collected in 2001–2, 12 percent of low-income respondents in three Argentine provinces received something from a political party in the election campaign that had occurred two months earlier. A study conducted in randomly selected villages in 12 municipalities in the Philippines finds that 14 percent of households receive goods from candidates prior to an election in exchange for voters (Cruz et al., 2021). Using various survey instruments, Muhtadi (2019) estimates that, in Indonesia, 25–35 percent of voters receive gifts meant to encourage them to vote for a candidate.

Thus, field research produces wide variation in the estimated frequency of campaign clientelism. There is an obvious difference between a population that reports that 10 percent of its members have been offered gifts in exchange for a vote from one where 40 percent reports this. Some of the difference may be explained by the use of different measurement strategies. But much of the difference remains to be explained. Overall, campaign clientelism could be considered moderately to very common today in many less developed countries.

Almost no studies quantify welfare clientelism, or the frequency with which officeholders respond to individual and collective welfare needs between elections. Perhaps this is because this figure normally approaches 100 percent. Elected politicians in every context respond to voter requests for assistance. "Constituency service" is a well-known and well-studied phenomenon in wealthy democracies (Cain et al., 1987). Of the three categories of individual welfare clientelism described above – (1) requests for information; (2) requests for discretionary goods or services; and (3) requests for illegitimate advantage – elected officials in developed democracies regularly engage in the the first; in the less developed countries, they regularly engage in the first two and are reported to also engage in the third. In other words, welfare clientelism is ubiquitous.

Of the three forms of welfare clientelism, we probably have the most information about requests for and provision of discretionary collective goods, especially basic infrastructure. In many developing countries, collective welfare clientelism for infrastructure development is baked into the system. Politicians are entitled to development funds from the central government in order to help their constituencies and they are typically given wide discretion in how they use the funds. Perhaps surprisingly, evidence shows that officeholders sometimes fail to properly operate the distribution of collective welfare clientelism. Studies of Indian officeholders report that many fail to use all the constituency development funds to which they are entitled, meaning that infrastructure projects that could have been built are not (Banerjee et al., 2011; Keefer & Khemani, 2009). Some scholars implicitly use the failure to spend out freely-available funds as evidence that campaign clientelism and welfare clientelism are substitutes; having engaged in vote buying before the election, they reason, politicians have no need to continue to buy votes after winning the seat.

However, there is little direct evidence to substantiate the view that politicians make these kinds of decisions. Instead, when officeholders fail to spend out all available funds in development projects, it may be due to difficulties in seeing constituency projects through to completion. Williams (2017) highlights that many projects remain unfinished not because of corruption or clientelism but because funds dry up before construction is completed. This suggests that politicians who could access development funds may not do so because even the funds available are inadequate for the projects of highest priority.

An alternative strand of literature sees welfare clientelism as displacing campaign clientelism as the vehicle of choice for politicians seeking to induce voter loyalty (Nichter, 2018). According to this view, the two types of clientelism are substitutes, perhaps emerging sequentially on a developmental path. An unanswered question is why and when politicians switch from one form of clientelism to the other.

But as we have already hinted, campaign and welfare clientelism need not be substitutes. A plausible interpretation of indiscriminate nonpartisan handouts in the preelectoral period is that they are meant to signal that the candidate will be good at welfare clientelism should he be elected (Kramon, 2018). If this is the case, then preelection and intra-election clientelism are complements. More campaign clientelism before the election is meant to signal more welfare clientelism after it. Corroborating this interpretation, a study set in Kenya finds that more investments in infrastructure projects occur in communities where the distribution of preelectoral handouts is highest (Kramon, 2018, p. 163).

Overall, the literature produces no clear interpretation of the underlying relationship between campaign and welfare clientelism. Thus, we do not know if interventions to reduce one will also reduce the other or instead push politicians to devote more resources to the alternative type of clientelism. What relevant evidence exists is scanty and probably case-specific. We encourage future work on this question.

4　Is Clientelism Effective? New Empirical Evidence

Like the literature, our review has so far focused on describing and interpreting clientelism. We now turn to a different problem, one that has been less deeply considered in existing scholarship. Is clientelism electorally effective? Does campaign clientelism actually secure votes? Is the discretionary distribution of services and public goods to voters by incumbents a useful way to gain electoral support?

To make progress in answering this question, we proceed as follows. We first present novel cross-national descriptive information on reelection rates of national legislators in the lower house. We probe the data to explore their robustness. We then compare the cross-national patterns to evidence gleaned from the existing case study literature. This comparison generates an apparent discrepancy between interpretations that emerge from the micro- and the macro-level data. To interrogate the discrepancy, in the following section we invoke interest group theory to explain why clientelism might be widespread even if it has only a limited electoral impact.

4.1　Clientelism and Reelection Rates

To evaluate the electoral effectiveness of clientelism, we first step back and examine the problem using an aggregate cross-national lens. We have collected data on the reelection rates of legislators in the lower house in as many democracies around the world as possible for the period 2000–18. Reelection rates are calculated by comparing the composition of a lower house legislature with its predecessor and counting the number of individuals serving in both. We then average the reelection rates across multiple elections whenever possible to eliminate idiosyncratic effects of particular electoral cycles. We have computed reelection rates for the period 2000–18 for 98 countries across the world. Countries included in the dataset are defined as democracies or as electoral autocracies in the 2000s; thus, we exclude countries classed by Varieties of Democracy (V-Dem) as "closed autocracies" in 2018. We impose two additional exclusion criteria. We omit countries with populations under 300,000 (in 2018), on the grounds that their outcomes might reflect external factors or that including them might bias our interpretation, at least unless we reweight observations by population. It is relatively standard in comparative political science to omit very small countries from many analyses for these reasons. We also omit countries that during the relevant period prohibit the reelection of legislators (such as Costa Rica, Ecuador, and Mexico for the period under consideration) (Carey, 1996).[13] Appendix A provides additional information on the construction of our reelection variable, and Appendix B describes the data sources.

Before presenting our findings, we discuss the limitations of this exercise and our reasons for engaging in it despite its weaknesses. One limitation of our approach is that we cannot distinguish legislators who exit the legislature due to actual electoral defeat from those who die, retire, withdraw, or are deselected by party leadership. This is because we do not have information on who runs, only on who wins and whose name then appears in the subsequent legislature. Without candidate lists, we necessarily merge various categories of the unelected into a single class.[14] Retirement and deselection decisions, however, are often strategic and a candidate who is likely to win is less likely to retire or to be removed. As such, although our measure underestimates reelection rates, the bias is more limited than may initially appear.

A second drawback to this exercise is that the evidence we present is descriptive and, as such, can only be indicative of whether clientelism is electorally effective or not. It is not causally valid to measure the effectiveness of clientelism by regressing politicians' reelection rates (or, if we had the data, vote shares) on their campaign or welfare clientelistic expenditures, which in essence is what we do below. The reason is that the choice of a strategy to convince voters – such as the use of clientelist inducements – is endogenous to

---

[13] However, we did not exclude the Philippines, although legislators there can serve only three consecutive three-year terms (Querubin, 2012, p. 3).

[14] Collecting data on members of parliament is possible using publicly available sources of data. The same is not the case for candidate lists, which often require direct requests to single political parties. Our data collection was confined to what we could gather from public domain sources.

politicians' characteristics and the situations (and voters) they face. This means that when we find a negative association between clientelism and reelection rates, we cannot know if this is because clientelism is ineffective or whether it is effective in gaining votes but simply inadequate to the objective circumstances confronting incumbents. Thus, the patterns that emerge in the data are consistent with the interpretation that clientelism is electorally ineffective – but they are not necessarily inconsistent with the reverse.

Nonetheless, we contend that the analysis below has value. One reason is that it is grounded in implicit theoretical predictions that arise out of a large body of literature. If clientelism were as effective as it is generally portrayed, we believe we should observe high reelection rates for politicians in the settings where it is most prevalent. Incumbent politicians enjoy regular access to the levers of government – access to which challengers are naturally denied – and are, thus, most likely to engage in clientelism, especially welfare clientelism.[15]

A second reason that we contend our analysis has value is that it resets scholarly obligations when undertaking micro-level field research on clientelism and political campaigns. Until release of the data in this study, research on clientelism took place in a macro-level vacuum. No one knew the macro-level patterns that might characterize reelection rates of all those politicians whose activities comprised the workings of clientelism. Now we know – as we show momentarily – that most national-level parliamentary politicians in the most clientelistic of environments fail to win reelection. This new fact introduces new micro-level research questions; in particular, it should require students of clientelist activities to study whether clientelism secures votes, and if not, why it persists. It raises questions, thus far unexplored, about the nature of electoral competition in clientelist contests. And, as we also discuss later, it introduces new questions about whether politicians may be heterogeneous in their clientelist activities and successes.

We now present data that allow us to answer a simple but empirically new question: at the aggregate level, are the data consistent with the theory that clientelism secures votes?

---

[15] Some, such as Vicente (2014, p. F377), suggest that preelectoral vote buying is concentrated among challengers to compensate for the absence of any record in providing welfare clientelism. The same argument is made by Kramon (2018), whose study of preelectoral handouts in Kenya finds that they are mainly used by challengers. However, such a view seems to us questionable. A large study conducted in Uganda reports that most vote buying is done by incumbent politicians rather than challengers (Blattman et al., 2019). An obvious reason is that incumbents enjoy consistent advantages in accessing government funds for preelectoral handouts. Thus, we suspect that incumbents are far more likely to use clientelism than challengers. However, we acknowledge that more empirical evidence is warranted on this point.

The cross-national data we have assembled exhibit a pattern that shows exactly the reverse of what this conjecture predicts. In Figure 1, we depict the relationship between a standard measure of clientelism and reelection rates for countries around the world. The measure of clientelism we use is based on the expert-coded data from the V-Dem project, documented in Coppedge et al. (2022, p. 295). We use this source because it is the most authoritative available for a large number of countries. The V-Dem project conceives of clientelism as an index of preelection vote buying, the distribution of particularistic rather

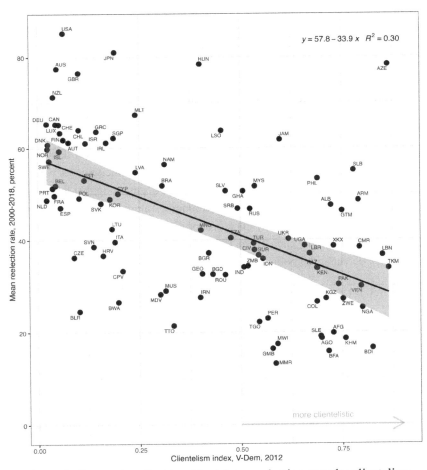

Figure 1 Scatterplot of national legislator reelection rates by clientelism index

Notes: Data from multiple elections where available (51 countries) and single elections otherwise (47 countries). N = 98 countries. Sources: Authors' calculations. Details on measures and data sources available in Appendices A and B.

than public goods, and clientelistic rather than programmatic party linkages. This is not identical to how we have conceptualized the phenomenon, but it is a plausible and relatively standard proxy and it captures parts of both campaign and welfare clientelism. The coding comes from experts and so has a large subjective component, which is why we suggest that readers interpret the results loosely. Nonetheless, the pattern that emerges from the data in Figure 1 is striking. It shows that as clientelism increases, *reelection rates fall*. The relationship is strong and extremely visible.

The relationship depicted in Figure 1 contrasts sharply with what the vast literature on clientelism implicitly imagines, which is that countries with high levels of clientelism should have high reelection rates. What good is all that supposed vote buying if it does not guarantee reelection? In the next section, we investigate whether some other factors might affect the simple correlation we have displayed so far.

Before proceeding, we note that Bowles and Marx (2022, fig. 1, p. 13) present similar reelection data for twelve African countries from the late 1990s and the 2000s. Those data confirm the existence of low reelection rates (40 percent and below) in all countries. Bowles and Marx (2022) also present data on the incumbent rerunning ratio, defined as the percentage of incumbents who run again. This varies from roughly 40 to 70 percent, documenting that low reelection rates may be accompanied by high rerunning rates, as is true in Malawi, Liberia, and Uganda. Thus, there is corroborative evidence for our contention that in countries where clientelism is endemic, incumbents may nonetheless experience defeat at the polls.

4.1.1 How Stable Is the Relationship between Clientelism and Reelection Rates?

The new data on reelection rates around the world that we present raise questions about the effectiveness of clientelism. If clientelism operates as expected, successfully luring voters to support candidates who provide handouts, why do we observe lower reelection rates for national legislators where clientelism is more prevalent?

Before turning to this question, we examine whether the observed relationship is stable in light of other obvious factors that might affect reelection rates. We do this mainly to satisfy curiosity, since we recognize that the cross-national relationship between clientelism and reelection rates that we have displayed cannot be interpreted as causal. And yet, it naturally suggests a causal relationship, one that we would like to investigate in the future using appropriate inferential methods. Because we cannot do that in the modest length of an Element, we probe the cross-national data that we have collected by considering the observed relationship in a multivariate setting – while fully aware that our analysis cannot be interpreted causally. Yet if we were to find that the association we have identified is easily swamped by other variables, we might be reluctant to pursue developing our analysis.

We incorporate one economic and two important institutional variables into the analysis: per capita income, party institutionalization, and district magnitude. Per capita national income is believed to be a confounding factor because it is held to drive clientelism. While we cannot untangle the relationship in this setting, we can at a minimum check how much the association between clientelism and reelection rates changes once we add per capita GDP into the equation. Party institutionalization is theoretically closely related to control over who enters politics as well as the operation of electoral competition. We examine whether clientelism is significantly associated with reelection rates even where political parties are more institutionalized. District magnitude, which captures the average number of representatives elected from each constituency, is also commonly believed to affect reelection rates. Rates are generally higher with smaller district magnitudes; thus, we explore whether district magnitude confounds the observed bivariate relationship between reelection rates and clientelism. Before presenting analytical results, we discuss in more detail the theory underlying inclusion of each variable.

Many students of clientelism contend that it emerges and then evaporates with industrialization (Scott, 1972; Stokes et al., 2013). If economic development drives clientelism, perhaps the process of modernization in turn changes reelection rates as polities acquire institutional resilience and stability. As one preliminary way to investigate this, we include a standard measure of per capita gross domestic product in our analysis.

How might political parties affect reelection rates? In developed democracies, candidates for legislative office are almost always selected by political parties. With their development, parties fundamentally transform the process of entry into the political realm (Aldrich, 1995). For electoral reasons, party leaders seek "better" individuals to run for office. In this context, better simply means that parties select candidates who are more likely to win. Various factors may contribute to the electoral success of certain candidates, and those factors may be context-specific. Perhaps the candidate is politically more experienced, better known among voters, or has some other particular characteristic that appeals to the electorate. Stronger parties, which exert more control over candidate selection, can better screen would-be politicians on those winning traits. Parties deliberately filter out weaker contenders, who are no longer free to contend elections simply because they choose to. Thus, where parties are more institutionalized, we should observe improved reelection rates – regardless of whether individual politicians engage in clientelistic practices or not. If party strength and clientelism are negatively correlated (as the V-Dem measure makes true by definition, an issue we consider momentarily), then the relationship we displayed in the previous subsection may be spurious.

We proxy the ability of political parties to directly affect reelection rates using V-Dem's index of party institutionalization. This measure incorporates (1) how stable party organizations are and (2) whether voters develop long-term connections with them (Bizzarro et al., 2017, p. 4). V-Dem constructs this as interval measures (based on a Bayesian item response model), where higher values mean more institutionalized parties. This is the single best proxy we have been able to locate that seems theoretically close to what we have in mind: the ability of parties to engineer higher reelection rates. However, the V-Dem index of clientelism includes at least one dimension that is also associated with party strength; namely, whether party linkages are clientelistic as opposed to programmatic (Coppedge et al., 2022, p. 295). The index of party institutionalization also incorporates the same measure (Coppedge et al., 2022, p. 315). As a result, the V-Dem measures of clientelism and of party institutionalization are correlated by construction, at least to some extent.

A second institutional variable that we bring in measures district magnitude. Empirically, the relationship between clientelism and reelection rates may be driven by characteristics of the electoral system. For instance, perhaps multimember constituencies reduce reelection rates compared with plurality electoral systems, independently of the degree of party system institutionalization. This might be because incumbents enjoy greater advantages in single-member districts, thanks to better name recognition among voters in districts with only one winner (Carey & Shugart, 1995; Shugart, 2005). If this were the case, legislatures elected from constituencies with smaller district magnitudes would be associated with higher reelection rates. To alleviate this concern, we include a measure of district magnitude (as of 2012). District magnitude corresponds to the average number of seats in each electoral constituency (or parliamentary district) for the lower house in a given country. It proxies a consistent measure capturing differences in electoral systems across countries.

We begin, as before, with graphic depictions. In Figure 2, we present a scatterplot of the relationship between the reelection rates of legislators to the lower house and per capita GDP for the same ninety-eight countries depicted in Figure 1. The data shown in the new figure document that reelection rates rise with national income and that poorer countries have lower reelection rates than

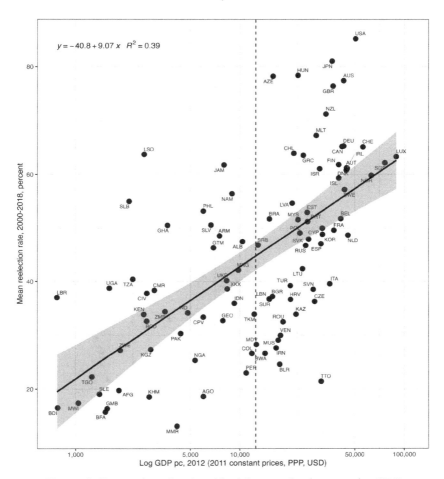

$y = -40.8 + 9.07\ x \quad R^2 = 0.39$

Figure 2 Scatterplot of national legislator reelection rates by GDP

Notes: Dashed vertical line divides low- and middle-income (left) from high-income (right), according to the World Bank's 2012 classification. Data from multiple elections where available (51 countries) and single elections otherwise (47 countries). N = 98 countries. Sources: Authors' calculations. Details on measures and data sources available in Appendices A and B.

wealthier ones. The average reelection rate of incumbents in the lower house in countries that the World Bank classes as low income (as of 2012) is only 27 percent, rising to 35 percent when we also include lower-middle-income countries. The average reelection rates is 52 percent in high-income nations. In other words, in low and middle-income countries, 65 percent of legislators who enter the lower house are challengers rather than incumbents. This association generates a concern that reelection rates that we have ascribed to clientelism might instead be driven by economic development, broadly conceived.

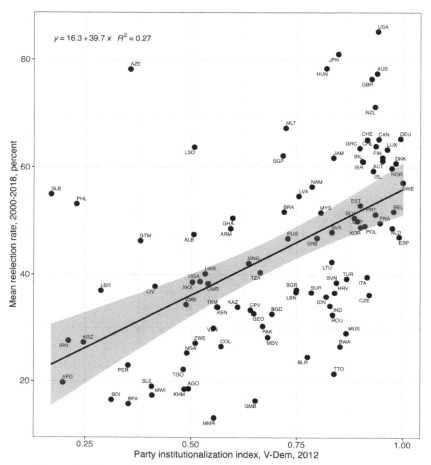

Figure 3 Scatterplot of national legislator reelection rates by party
institutionalization index

Notes: Data from multiple elections where available (51 countries) and single elections otherwise
(47 countries). N = 98 countries. Sources: Authors' calculations. Details on measures and data
sources available in Appendices A and B.

We show the bivariate relationship between the V-Dem measure of party
institutionalization and reelection rates in Figure 3. The figure shows that the
data behave as we would expect: reelection rates rise with more party institutionalization. The relationship is quite pronounced. If we were constructing a
causal argument, we would worry that some of the impact of clientelism might
in fact derive from party institutionalization.

Finally, in Figure 4, we present a scatterplot of the log of district magnitude
against reelection rates. We use the V-Dem measure of average district magnitude for the seats in the lower chamber of the legislature (as of 2012). The figure

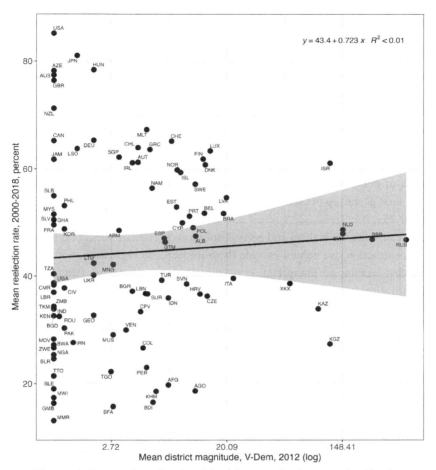

Figure 4 Scatterplot of national legislator reelection rates by district magnitude

Notes: Data from multiple elections where available (51 countries) and single elections otherwise (47 countries). N = 98 countries. Sources: Authors' calculations. Details on measures and data sources available in Appendices A and B.

shows no relationship between the two variables; not surprisingly, the statistical relationship between reelection rates and district magnitude is insignificant at conventional thresholds. Although this does not rule out any potential causal importance of the electoral system for reelection rates, no obvious correlation exists across countries.

To continue this preliminary data analysis, we now present regression results using the variables we study. The regressions feature reelection rates across countries as the dependent variable, the V-Dem measure of clientelism, per capita GDP, the institutionalization of the party system, and district magnitude as regressors. The inclusion of the three new variables that we conceive of as controls allows us to assess whether clientelism appears to exercise an independent effect on reelection rates when parties are more institutionalized, when district magnitude is greater, and at the same level of GDP.

Results reported in Table 1 highlight that once we control for GDP, the relationship between clientelism and reelection rates becomes substantively and statistically weaker, as is evident in column 2. When we control for GDP, clientelism remains negatively associated with reelection rates, but the relationship is not statistically significant at standard levels. This is probably because the index of clientelism is very strongly correlated with economic development, measured as the log of GDP per capita, with a Pearson's correlation coefficient of -0.75.

Because the clientelism and party institutionalization indices are correlated by construction, we cannot include them in the same regression, nor can we put any meaningful interpretation on the size of their effects. Party institutionalization, when included in addition to per capita GDP (column 3), does not have a statistically significant effect on reelection rates. In column 4, we show the effect of district magnitude and clientelism on reelection rates, without including per capita GDP. District magnitude has no significant association with reelection rates.

The final column of regression results reported in Table 1 shows results with the inclusion of clientelism, per capita GDP, and district magnitude. Clientelism is still negatively associated with reelection rates, but the relationship is no longer statistically significant. District magnitude is negatively associated with reelection rates, suggesting that smaller electoral districts – for instance, single-member districts – experience higher reelection rates. Similar to the effects of GDP, we cannot parcel out the effects of party institutionalization and the log of district magnitude, which show a Pearson's correlation coefficient of 0.19.

The analysis we have just presented consistently finds that clientelism is negatively related to reelection rates, although the coefficient for clientelism does not always achieve statistical significance. These findings also highlight that economic development is strongly associated with reelection rates. As countries develop economically, incumbents become more likely to succeed in retaining their seats. This introduces new questions about whether there may be differences in the characteristics of who enters politics at different levels of economic development, questions that our study asks but does not answer. For now, we note that our main statistical finding is that clientelism is negatively related to reelection rates across countries even taking into account other possibly relevant variables.

Table 1 Regression results for the correlation between clientelism index and reelection rates

			Reelection rates		
	(1)	(2)	(3)	(4)	(5)
Clientelism, 2012	−33.865***	−11.177		−34.363***	−10.028
	(5.564)	(8.551)		(5.658)	(8.413)
GDP p.c., 2012 (log)		7.123***	8.002***		8.035***
		(1.873)	(2.016)		(2.013)
Party institutionalization, 2012			7.153		
			(12.042)		
District magnitude, 2012 (log)				−0.494	−1.738*
				(0.877)	(0.934)
Constant	57.813***	−18.076	−35.827***	58.689***	−24.708
	(2.469)	(20.364)	(12.301)	(3.364)	(20.945)
N	98	98	98	98	98
Adjusted R²	0.289	0.391	0.380	0.284	0.405

Notes: ***Significant at the 1 percent level.
**Significant at the 5 percent level.
*Significant at the 10 percent level.
Robust standard errors in parentheses.

4.1.2 Possible Qualifications to Our Argument

Except in passing, the existing case study literature on clientelism has not explicitly analyzed whether it successfully promotes the reelection of legislators. Yet it seems to be an assumption among students of clientelism that it *ought* to promote reelection; thus, scholars may be taken aback by the implications of the patterns in the data we presented above. There are various ways that readers could reconcile the cross-national patterns we have just presented with the idea that clientelism is nonetheless electorally effective. We now discuss two that emerge from existing literature: the first having to do with possible differences between party leaders and backbenchers and the second with differences between the legislature and other levels of government.

The idea that there may be consequential differences in reelection rates between party leaders and backbenchers hinges on possible discrepancies between aggregate and subgroup reelection rates. Although aggregate reelection rates across countries are lower where clientelism is generally higher, average national-level data may not tell a fully accurate story. Clientelism operates at the level of individual politicians in their interactions with voters. The data that are shown in Figures 1 and 2 are at the level of national legislatures. The data in the figures could thereby disguise an "ecological fallacy," or a misalignment between the pattern that emerges from aggregate data and the behavior of the individuals (or subgroups of individuals) that comprise the aggregate.

Successful clientelistic practices may be the preserve of a handful of powerful party leaders rather than a generalized practice used by all candidates – or even all incumbents – for public office. Maybe all candidates try to operate their election campaigns via clientelism but only those with the greatest resources succeed in buying enough votes to win. This view acknowledges that most legislators do not get reelected precisely because they lack sufficient resources to use clientelism effectively and buy enough voters; clientelism is ineffective because of inadequate distributive resources. Only a select elite is able to leverage access to government resources, engage in sufficiently extensive campaign clientelism, and thereby secure reelection. Indeed, the same elite may deliberately deny less powerful politicians access to the resources they need to achieve electoral success and prevent them from gaining renomination, precisely in order to reinforce its own control.

There is some empirical evidence that supports this interpretation. Analyzing data from thirteen sub-Saharan African countries, Warren (2019) contends that this is the case in many of these countries. Additional, albeit indirect, evidence in support of this view comes from a study of the growth of assets of Indian politicians. Only a small minority, comprised mainly of government ministers, experience unusual asset growth while in office, with most state-level legislators unable to convert political position into wealth (Fisman et al., 2014). Thus, in India, most legislators may not amass sufficient funds to engage in ongoing electoral clientelism.[16] Similarly, A. Lee (2020) reports that candidates affiliated with less centralized Indian political parties do not experience an incumbency disadvantage whereas those affiliated with centralized parties – where candidate nomination is controlled by party leaders – face an incumbency disadvantage. Thus, where party leaders control the candidate nomination process, they may leverage their resources to systematically deny reelection to backbenchers. We have not been able to locate more data that would allow us to investigate separately the reelection rates of backbenchers and elite politicians across or even within other countries, however, preventing us from investigating this argument in other settings. As a result, we have no way to know how general these patterns are.

A second argument is that national legislators might be the wrong office-holders to study. In some countries, discretionary resources appear to be largely under the control of politicians operating at levels of government other than the national legislature. This is especially true for countries where presidential power is very strong and where legislatures are subservient to the executive branch. For instance, many Latin American countries are known for strong executives, regional governments, and local governments – but weak national legislatures. Perhaps clientelism is politically effective for the politicians operating at these other levels even if it is not for national legislators. In accordance with this view, the extensive literature on clientelism in Latin America is focused largely on local-level political party machines (Calvo & Murillo, 2004; Nichter, 2008; Szwarcberg, 2015). It is unclear whether this is because local politics is principally where scholars contend that clientelism takes place or because it is easier for researchers to access local politics. Especially for solo scholars, it is feasible to observe and collect data on local politics but perhaps more difficult logistically to jump across legislative constituencies to observe and collect data on national-level parliamentarians. Collecting observational information about clientelist practices on the ground for national legislators would be helpful, just as looking at reelection rates of local and

---

[16] The study uses a regression discontinuity research design, comparing asset growth of near-winners with that of near-losers. Presumably due to the reduction in sample size that arises, there is no attempt to estimate the relationship between asset growth and subsequent reelection probabilities.

national politicians separately would help to refine our understanding of the effectiveness of clientelism. Yet, again, the necessary data are not available.

More broadly, many studies of clientelism are relatively vague about the level of the politicians who operate the levers of discretionary disbursements. Studies of local politics sometimes fail to discuss explicitly whether national politicians are involved in the clientelistic networks that they depict, or they appear to implicitly assume that what they observe at the local level is paralleled at other levels of the political system. We suspect this is because prior work has failed to ask explicitly about the levels and types of political actors who may be involved in clientelism, or whether clientelism at one level of the political system is necessarily replicated throughout.

Two of the best studied historical country cases of clientelism are Mexico and Italy, which exhibit admixtures of the two features we have just mentioned: party elites advantaged by resources and strong nonlegislative political actors. Both countries experienced long-term single-party dominance which scholars ascribe to successful ongoing clientelist practices (Chubb, 1982; Magaloni, 2006). Does the evidence from these cases contradict our argument about ineffective clientelism? We think not, although these cases certainly carry interesting nuances. In twentieth-century Mexico, during the long reign of the Institutional Revolutionary Party, legislators were prohibited legally from serving more than a single term. By definition, then, the reelection rate was zero; by construction, party elites prevented legislators from amassing any incumbency advantage. In postwar Italy, only a tiny elite in the dominant Christian Democratic Party enjoyed any incumbency advantage, whereas the bulk of deputies elected over the second half of the twentieth century served only one or two terms (Golden & Picci, 2015). In both countries, a dominant party successfully remained in power over many decades despite the fact that all or most legislators were not reelected. Clientelist practices may have been deployed to buttress political dominance, but the average legislator was not engaging in them or at least not to his own direct political advantage. Especially in the context of our new cross-national evidence, we see that although clientelism was highly visible in Mexico and Italy, it was confined to nonlegislative political actors or to a tiny number of legislators. Pinpointing the actors who successfully engaged in clientelist practices also leads us to ask what other features of the political system may have contributed to long-term single-party dominance in Mexico and Italy.

Of course, there is likely to be genuine variation across countries and regions in the level at which clientelistic practices take place and in the actors involved. Perhaps in some countries, only party leaders control enough resources to engage successfully in clientelism. Perhaps in others, successful clientelism is the prerogative of the executive. We think these questions are important. But we note that they arise by virtue of the patterns revealed by our data: national legislators face lower reelection rates in countries where clientelism is generally prevalent.[17] And we encourage research specifically into these questions.

Before turning to theoretical literature that we believe provides a strong explanation of the pattern our data uncover, in the next section we turn to studies that have looked into the effectiveness of clientelism within a single country or in a handful of countries.

4.2 Case Study Evidence on the Effectiveness of Clientelism

As others have noted, only a handful of studies seek to put precise numbers on the electoral returns of vote buying and clientelism (Cantú, 2019). Most of those that look at the effectiveness of vote buying do so in isolation from other campaign activities. That is, the object of scrutiny is vote buying specifically rather than the full array of activities that take place during an electoral campaign. Taken on its own, the effects of clientelism appear to be in line with the evidence presented in the previous section: vote buying efforts are not very effective. An analysis of national survey data from Brazil in 2010 reports that a fifth of voters admit to having receiving an election handout – but to little avail when it comes to their vote choice:

> Citizens who reported receiving vote buying offers during recent elections were asked whether their latest offer increased or decreased their inclination to vote for the politician or party who offered the benefit. Clientelist offers were apparently not very effective: only 18 percent indicated they were more inclined to vote for the politician, whereas 44 percent indicated they were less inclined and 38 percent remained the same. (Nichter, 2018, p. 95)

---

[17] Notice that we only refer to low reelection rates rather than to "incumbency disadvantage" or "incumbency effect." Our data do not allow us to measure these quantities. An incumbency advantage or disadvantage (such as that studied by A. Lee [2020] in India and just discussed) refers to whether a candidate has greater or lower chances to win the election when he runs as an incumbent. The incumbency effect refers to the electoral gains or losses induced solely by virtue of being in office, everything else equal. The most commonly used method to measure the incumbency effect, pioneered in political settings by D. S. Lee (2008), is to compare close winners and close losers at the level of the political party using a regression discontinuity design. Our data are not suitable for such a research design because we only have information about winners and because we lack data on vote shares. We suspect that the pattern that we observe of a failure to gain reelection by incumbents in the less developed countries of the world is likely to reflect a generalized incumbency disadvantage there, but we cannot be certain. For evidence on the incumbency effect in specific countries, see Linden (2004); Uppal (2009) on India, Klašnja and Titiunik (2017) on Brazilian mayors, and Eggers and Spirling (2017) on historical Britain.

In analyses of surveys in Benin and four other countries (Kenya, Mali, Botswana, and Uganda), Guardado and Wantchekon (2018) show that handouts appear to have no effect on voters' turnout or vote choices. Rather than clientelism per se, the authors argue that it is the general competitive environment that explains electoral outcomes. Similarly, an analysis of 17 elections in sub-Saharan Africa between 2000 and 2005 finds that although vote buying increases turnout, in only a single election in a single country did it translate into an electoral advantage (Guardado & Wantchekon, 2021). Muhtadi (2019) and Aspinall et al. (2017) show in the context of Indonesia that many gifts go to waste politically. Although we do not know how voters would have voted absent handouts, these studies report that between 40 and 85 percent of handouts fail to win a vote in return.[18] Thus, in the few studies to have asked whether vote buying actually buys votes, the answer seems to be that it does not.

The picture changes, however, when the effects of clientelism are directly compared with those deriving from alternative campaign activities. When examined in relation to the main alternative – promises of public policies in the interest of broad groups of voters – clientelism emerges as relatively effective. In a path-breaking field experiment conducted in Benin, Wantchekon (2003) randomizes candidates' campaign promises to voters. In some villages, candidates campaign on a public goods platform (reform of the national education and health systems); in others, on a welfare clientelistic platform (provision of roads and patronage jobs). Wantchekon finds that clientelistic platforms are more successful than platforms focused on national policy programs. Cruz et al. (2018) use a structural model to study the impact of information about politicians' promises and accomplishments on voters' propensities to vote for a candidate in the Philippines. The study finds that with the right information, voters are able to evaluate performance and vote accordingly. That is, voters successfully engage in retrospective voting and electorally reward good performance while in office. However, the study also reports that voters with clientelistic ties to politicians are less likely to respond to information about performance. In addition, the authors contend that vote buying is a more efficient tool than alternative campaign activities. The number of votes obtained per-dollar-spent outweighs disseminating information about past achievements and future commitments.

The conclusion that clientelism gains more votes than programmatic alternatives is also in line with the findings of studies on the electoral consequences

---

[18] An exception to this assessment of the electoral impact of clientelism is found in Stokes (2005, p. 321), which states that a large part of Argentine voters who admitted to having received a handout changed their vote as a result. This result seems anomalous, however.

of programmatic transfers. Diaz-Cayeros et al. (2016) examine the adoption of a formula-based poverty program to replace the discretionary distribution of poverty relief in Mexico. The analysis finds that the distribution of discretionary goods to individuals has larger electoral payoffs than the discretionary allocation of infrastructure goods. While temporal asymmetries prevent a direct comparison between the electoral returns from discretionary goods to individuals and those from more programmatic policies, results from the study suggest that the former are probably larger (p. 181).[19] Similarly, Imai et al. (2020) report a null effect of the adoption of programmatic policies on incumbent electoral fortunes in Mexico.

The low electoral reward provided by the transition to programmatic policies has various possible causes. In Imai et al. (2020), programmatic policies are adopted by a cross-party coalition, thereby preventing candidate differentiation. If multiple parties band together to support programmatic policies, support is not useful for gaining votes. Alternatively, programmatic policies may be poorly implemented due to low bureaucratic expertise (Diaz-Cayeros et al., 2016; Geddes, 1994). In this case, voters may not receive the benefits promised. Campaigning on programmatic promises when the policies cannot be delivered will naturally encounter voter disbelief; it is accordingly difficult for even theoretically willing politicians to switch strategies. Finally, programmatic policies may be electorally valuable for attracting floating voters (Asunka, 2017), who may otherwise be out of the party's reach (Keefer & Vlaicu, 2008). But in many environments, especially those marked by ethnic or ideological polarization, there may not be many floating voters to attract. Whatever the reason, the outcome seems the same. Political parties may postpone adopting programmatic policies because clientelism is so much more effective in the short term for winning elections. Clientelist practices appear to be extremely sticky and difficult to undo.

If studies that compare vote buying to programmatic promises show the short-term electoral superiority of the former, the same is not the case for studies that compare vote buying to violence and intimidation. Violence turns out to be less expensive and more successful than clientelism: where violence can be used, it discourages opposition supporters from going to the polls more effectively than gifts to potential supporters induce them to turn out and vote as hoped (Gonzalez-Ocantos et al., 2020). However, there are few environments where it is feasible to use violence as an electoral strategy – many fewer than those where clientelism and vote buying may be used. Government security

---

[19] According to our definition of clientelism, both types of disbursements would be classed as clientelism because both are discretionary and aimed at gaining votes.

forces need to overlook the use of violence, and violence needs to be deployed in opposition strongholds or it risks intimidating one's own electoral supporters. Even more than clientelism – which in some circumstances induces backlash (Carlin & Moseley, 2021) – violence is a high-risk strategy, and one that is less widely adopted.

Overall, therefore, there is mixed case study evidence about the effectiveness of clientelism. On average, clientelism seems to exhibit limited effectiveness in achieving its goals – although somewhat paradoxically, the little empirical evidence that has been collected suggests that it remains more effective for politicians in the short term than switching to programmatic policy commitments. This introduces a dilemma for politicians involved in vote buying: clientelism is not very effective, but any realistic immediate alternative may be worse. In the next section, we draw on interest group theory to provide an explanation for why clientelism is both prevalent and not particularly effective.

5 An Interest Group Interpretation of the Prevalence of Clientelism

In this section, we untangle the apparent paradox generated by our data: clientelism is most common in the countries where apparently it is least effective. To understand how clientelism can be widespread even if it is of little help electorally, we invoke well-known mechanisms from interest group theory.

Other scholars of clientelism have already suggested that it resembles a prisoner's dilemma (Chauchard, 2018; Hicken & Nathan, 2020; Muhtadi, 2019; Nathan, 2019). Like any prisoner's dilemma, clientelism diminishes the welfare of all involved – politicians as well as voters – but continues to be used because it is the best strategy available for each actor.

To understand the fundamental logic of this, we invoke the framework developed in Grossman and Helpman (2001). It presents similar dilemmas that confront interest groups using campaign contributions to lobby politicians for policy favors. When only one interest group seeks to buy policies using campaign contributions, it tilts the politician's platform in its preferred direction. But when two opposing lobbies compete with each other, their efforts cancel each other out (Grossman & Helpman, 2001). The intuition is obvious: when a politician receives donations from opposing lobbies which are competing to buy influence over policy, he accepts both campaign contributions while remaining beholden to neither.

The phenomenon of lobbying by interest groups serves as an analogue to vote buying by politicians. If only one candidate provides gifts to voters, doing so gives him an electoral bonus. But if all candidates do so, each gains some votes but loses other votes to equally generous competitors. The overall outcome is that campaign clientelism barely affects electoral results at all.

Does this mean a candidate for office can desist from engaging in campaign clientelism? If one candidate, perhaps taking the moral high ground, refrains from providing handouts when her opponent continues to do so, she will suffer certain defeat.[20] The best response to the fact that her electoral opponent buys votes is to buy votes herself. And indeed, if none of her opponents provides handouts, a candidate would find giving voters gifts a profitable campaign strategy because it would significantly improve her electoral chances. Obviously, if all candidates reason in this way, all engage in campaign clientelism. In equilibrium, therefore, all candidates would be better off if none were to engage in campaign clientelism but all find it optimal to hand out gifts to constituents. The situation thus mirrors a pure prisoner's dilemma. Even if political candidates wish they could stop clientelistic handouts before an election, they are all trapped into continuing to provide them.

Considered in this light, clientelism is both wasteful and persistent. Money is wasted on brokers because other politicians also pay brokers. Money is wasted on voters because other candidates also buy votes. Money is wasted on gifts because other candidates offer voters gifts. Political parties and candidates would all benefit putting an end to this waste while campaigning. But they cannot without placing themselves at a political disadvantage.

We have already referred to empirical studies that support the view that clientelism often appears to be the best strategy available to those who seek public office. These studies are entirely consistent with the theoretical logic of a prisoner's dilemma. We have also highlighted recent studies that show that reassuring voters that their votes are secret is not enough to change candidate behavior (even if it changes how voters cast their ballots) (Arias et al., 2019; Blattman et al., 2019; Vasudevan, 2019; Vicente, 2014). Thus, even when apparently offered an opportunity to shift away from clientelism in the electoral period, candidates exhibit unwillingness to do so. When we consider campaign clientelism a prisoner's dilemma, it is clear why.

The empirical evidence offered by the literature that we have reviewed in this Element does not bode well for the hope that politicians themselves are

---

[20] Of course, this depends on a competitive electoral environment, as we have already noted. In a highly lopsided race, where one candidate has a large built-in advantage, the disadvantaged might refrain from vote buying. Given that she is bound to lose, this hardly matters. Grossman and Helpman (2001) consider various interesting amendments along these lines that we do not pursue here.

appropriately positioned to end or even significantly reduce campaign clientelism. Instead, they are locked into providing useless gifts and treats for voters.

5.1 Interpreting Welfare Clientelism

The above discussion of a prisoner's dilemma offers little guidance for interpreting welfare clientelism, which does not easily fit into the setup of a prisoner's dilemma. Welfare clientelism typically takes place under the auspices of a single incumbent. In welfare clientelism, the key players are officeholders, bureaucrats, and others who do the bidding of politicians, and constituents. The first tries to manipulate her reputation and, therefore, her chances of reelection.[21] Voters try to ascertain whether the politician will deliver requested goods and services; that is, whether the politician is reliably committed to improving the welfare of citizens or is simply an unreliable opportunist or ineffective operative.

As Fearon (1999) shows, once we include differences in ability between candidates, voters base their electoral decision on this distinction. That is, if politicians are not identical, elections serve as an instrument to select the better candidate rather than as a way to reward good performance.[22] The operation of welfare clientelism affords the incumbent repeated opportunities to impress voters that he is personally more committed to improving their welfare and that he alone can reliably be expected to continue delivering the personal assistance they require. Thus, welfare clientelism allows the incumbent to attempt to construct a personally loyal electorate. Like campaign clientelism, welfare clientelism proves a persistent behavior for each incumbent in his search for a secure vote base.

Will ongoing welfare clientelism lead to reelection of the incumbent? If voters expect politicians to supply welfare goods, they discount their delivery when they evaluate the incumbent's performance. Attempts to create a loyal clientele fail when voters see such provisions as their due and understand it as part of the incumbent's job rather than as personal favor. Thus, it provides no electoral advantage but cannot be dispensed with. Not providing assistance will cause the officeholder to lose the next election, but providing it does not ensure success. Incumbents are trapped by the expectations of their voters.

---

[21] We do not theorize the independent behavior of the second here, assuming instead that bureaucrats simply follow the instructions of elected politicians. For recent work that begins to untangle the different incentives and behaviors of the bureaucrats and the politicians that supervise them, see Martin and Raffler (2020); Slough (2021).

[22] A useful discussion is Dewan and Shepsle (2011, pp. 324–5). For some empirical evidence that supports the contention that elections screen candidates rather than evaluate past performance, see Gagliarducci and Nannicini (2013); Galasso and Nannicini (2011).

5.2 Implications for Policy Remedies to Reduce Clientelism

In the previous sections, we have invoked mechanisms drawn from formal theory to reconcile the fact that although campaign and welfare clientelism are widespread, neither leads to high reelection rates. Both campaign and welfare clientelism are undone by the actions of others, whether the actions of other candidates or of citizens. Vote buying is undone by electoral competition, whereas the provision of public goods by an incumbent fails to manipulate voters' evaluations of the incumbent. In both cases, reelection rates may have little to do with what politicians do while running for or serving in public office, even while politicians cannot break with inefficient types of behavior.

Both campaign and welfare clientelism are economically and politically distortionary. Yet they are unlikely to disappear on their own. Political actors are not able to select a better equilibrium; instead, they operate under "perverse" incentives that make each of them better off engaging in clientelism, even though all of them would ideally prefer to desist from it. For public policy or legislation to successfully reduce campaign or welfare clientelism, it must affect politicians' payoffs. We suggest two policy modifications that could achieve this: strengthening the judiciary and facilitating the entry of new political parties.

An independent and active judiciary is a well-known instrument for exposing corruption. Events in Brazil illustrate the judiciary's potential role. Under President Luiz Inácio Lula da Silva, the Brazilian federal government initiated random audits of municipal accounts with the aim of reducing corruption (Ferraz & Finan, 2008). The hope was that voters would hold mayors accountable for siphoning off funds; in the end, electoral punishment was limited and hinged on idiosyncratic features of the municipality, such as the presence of a local radio station. Nonetheless, the main success of audits was due to the judiciary (Avis et al., 2018). By making sure that the acts of corruption that it revealed did not go unpunished, the judiciary exercised disciplinary effects on mayors.

The judicial channel has other advantages. Judges may not have to wait for politicians to act and in some settings may move independently of them. This was the case with *Lava Jato*, the massive corruption scandal involving the Brazilian state-owned oil company, Petrobras, that began in 2014. As Prado (2021) explains, the judiciary initiated its investigations by reinterpreting corrupt acts, applying rules of association to political parties that had previously been used to target criminal organizations, and using the police to forcibly bring suspects before a judge. The example shows the extraordinary role the judiciary may assume in initiating political change, a role similar to that played previously by the Italian judiciary in the early 1990s (Fisman & Golden, 2017, ch. 8).

An independent judiciary thus has the power to change the incentives under which politicians operate by exogenously increasing the costs for engaging in clientelism and corruption. Yet there are also multiple challenges to an effective judiciary. There needs to be clear public and professional support for novel judicial interventions aimed at reining in corruption and clientelism. Returning to the *Lavo Jato* case, protests by jurists against the reinterpretation of existing jurisprudence empowered interest groups; a similar reaction took place in Italy following the *Mani Pulite* exposure of corruption in the 1990s. In both cases, after an initial burst of activity, political reactions against what was seen as judicial overreach curtailed judicial independence. And finally, the tools of the judiciary need to be adapted to counter campaign clientelism. This is difficult since campaign clientelism is less likely to leave a paper trail than other types of corrupt activities by politicians, such as accepting bribes from companies in exchange for awarding a public contract. Exposing campaign clientelism might be easier if there were regulations around campaign spending, perhaps followed by audits that track campaign expenses, for instance. But even then, it will not be easy; evading such regulations is common practice.

A more radical way to change the incentives of politicians may occur when a new political party comes on the scene. If a new political party emerges that selects candidates untainted by prior involvement in clientelism and determined to avoid such activities, this can alter the payoffs to existing parties. In recent years, Mexico, India, Pakistan, and Romania have all witnessed the emergence of new anti-clientelistic and anti-corruption parties. These new entrants stake their reputations on their determination to upend established clientelistic and corrupt ways of doing politics. They introduce new modes of electoral competition and threaten the ability of dominant parties to protect the status quo. Their entry into the political realm may reduce the electoral benefits from engaging in campaign clientelism, a necessary condition for limiting the use of such tactics. Of course, for this to occur, political entrepreneurs need to have incentives to enter the electoral arena. They need a base of funding, one which is independent of political corruption – thus, possibly dependent on remittances from expatriates. The fear of reprisal must be largely absent, meaning that the risk of electoral violence must be limited or absent. Finally, new entrants must expect voters to support their endeavor.

For widespread public support to emerge that actively opposes existing clientelist practices, the press needs to broadcast political wrongdoing (Chang et al., 2010; Glaeser & Goldin, 2006). Civil society organizations need to shame politicians. A large number of citizens need to reject clientelistic practices, a process that becomes more likely to occur as a middle class emerges with economic development (Weitz-Shapiro, 2014). Citizen groups need to press for electoral and possibly judicial reform. Organizations need to support the judiciary against the pushback of powerful interest groups. Institutional solutions help but are insufficient to substantially change the payoffs from campaign clientelism. Citizens have an active role to play.

Welfare clientelism needs to be replaced by programmatic policies that permit the development of a true welfare state. In the case of welfare clientelism, there is some historical evidence that politicians may shift to programmatic policies even in the absence of external pressures. In some cases, intense competition among political parties has pressed existing political elites to reform the public bureaucracy and institute meritocratic recruitment criteria, thereby laying the groundwork for a more impartial and efficient distribution of government goods and services between elections. Geddes (1994) makes this argument in her interpretation of civil service reform in Latin America, for instance. In other cases, pressure from outside the political system is reported to be crucial. Such pressure may arise from organized business interests, which find clientelism and patronage increasingly unpalatable to their need for a meritocratic and efficient public bureaucracy (Kuo, 2018), or from an international actor which is embarrassed by the clientelist and corrupt politics of a client state (Manion, 2004).

Because welfare clientelism and campaign handouts operate in distinct arenas, at different times, and sometimes are aimed at different groups of citizens, curtailing one may do little to reduce the other. Indeed, reducing welfare clientelism by substituting in programmatic policies may even have the paradoxical effect of encouraging more campaign clientelism. Catalinac and Muraoka (2021) provide an example of unintended consequences along these lines. They find that candidates offer more clientelistic goods to voters in Japanese localities that receive state subsidies – in this case, subsidies for snow removal – than in localities that did not. Programmatic policies, by improving voter welfare, make voters more expensive to "buy" without changing the incentives of politicians to use gifts to attract voters when they campaign for reelection. We have no way to know if this is a general feature of the relationship between campaign and welfare clientelism. But we caution that activities to reduce one may do nothing to reduce the other and that policy needs to be directed separately at each.

Clientelism is a complicated phenomenon with multiple facets that requires a multifaceted approach to accelerate its demise. We use the term "acceleration" on purpose. In the next and final section of this Element, we remind readers that clientelism never fully disappears; instead, it evolves with economic development.

6 Rethinking Clientelism and Development

Our Element makes three main points. First, new national-level data on reelection rates from many countries around the world introduce unanswered questions about the electoral effectiveness of clientelism. Second, clientelism represents a prisoner's dilemma and thus may be widely employed even when it is not electorally beneficial to those engaging in it. And finally, we suggest that clientelism be defined as the discretionary distribution of resources by politicians. In this final section, we extend these points as a way to guide the future study of clientelism.

6.1 Clientelism and Development

We begin our discussion with our definition of clientelism. Over time, it has become less controversial to claim that we would be intellectually better off if we agreed to remove the notion of contingency from the concept of clientelism. In Section 3.1, we laid out the theoretical and practical issues raised by assuming that clientelistic exchanges are contingent interactions in which politicians give voters something in in exchange for electoral support. Here, we explore some benefits of adopting the perspective that we endorse.

Defining clientelism as the discretionary use by politicians of resources for electoral purposes allows us to connect political practices across developing and developed democracies. A large literature studies what are called pork-barrel politics – the discretionary use of government funding for infrastructure projects – in richer countries. In the United States, Berry et al. (2010) show that the president distributes more funds he controls to electoral districts that are represented by copartisans than those represented by his partisan opponents. Gordon (2011) describes how the administration of President George W. Bush manipulated expenditures by the General Service Administration to improve the electoral fortunes of Republican candidates to Congress in the subsequent elections. In neither of these examples is contingency part of the story. In the 2020 presidential primary campaign, Michael Bloomberg attempted to woo voters with food (Eater, 2020), apparently with little success (as our analysis of campaign clientelism would suggest). How different are these practices from what scholars of developing countries observe when they study campaign clientelism?

There is certainly a family resemblance. Indeed, we contend that clientelism does not ever entirely disappear, although it becomes less visible and more organized with the development of large-scale modern democratic political institutions. Rather, clientelism evolves with economic growth. We propose four stages to roughly delineate the historical development of clientelism. The first is the phase of the traditional patron–client hierarchies that bound landlord and tenant across much of the rural world prior to the introduction of the suffrage, and that lingers today in the form of coercive clientelism even after the lower classes have received the right to vote (Mares, 2015; Mares & Young, 2019; Mohmand, 2019). This relationship derives from the limited outside economic options of clients, which renders them dependent on their patrons. As a country develops economically, agricultural workers gradually benefit from economic opportunities outside their rural locality, changing the balance of power in the relationship between tenant and landlord (for a description of this phenomenon in Pakistan, see Mohmand [2019]). At this point, clientelism enters what we demarcate as a second phase.

In this second phase, the patron is no longer the landlord but the electoral boss. Suffrage is universal and voters acquire some bargaining power, but deficits in the establishment of the rule of law still leave political parties, candidates, and their agents with more power. The ballot may still not be secret or may be secret only in principle. This is the period when vote buying is at its peak, because electoral organizations easily control the electorate. This is also the period when electoral actors can, and therefore do, make use of contingency. This is the period known by the operation of the political machine (Scott, 1972).

As government bureaucracies develop along with the fiscal capacity of the state, a third phase emerges. It is characterized by the increasing absence of contingency, in which clientelism comes to resemble a discretionary and incomplete welfare state (Diaz-Cayeros et al., 2007; Geddes, 1994). Much of the research into clientelism that has taken place in the last decade that has been conducted by political scientists is based in settings that are, we believe, experiencing this phase – the post-independence states of Africa and Asia, and parts of Latin America. Europe underwent this phase at the end of nineteenth and early twentieth centuries and much can be learned from this history – much more than research has uncovered thus far. In Europe and Britain, this epoch was marked by the development of mutual aid societies, working-class political parties, and trade unions. These organizations emerged in the first instance to provide what we are calling welfare clientelism to their constituents. Uprooted from rural society, industrial workers in Europe were without the natural supports of the agrarian environment; new organizations stepped into the void to provide basic insurance in the form of funeral benefits, old age and widow's pensions, and compensation for loss of income and the costs of medical treatment during sickness. The working-class organizations that developed to carry out these tasks leveraged the delivery of social services to inculcate reluctant and apolitical low-income citizens with socialist thinking. In order to increase their electoral appeal, responsibility for providing welfare benefits was taken up by working-class parties once they became legal. The Germany Social Democratic Party was at the time perhaps the best known European socialist party for its engagement with what we are calling welfare clientelism (Roth, 1963). That trade unions still distribute unemployment insurance in a handful of European countries is a visible remnant of this process (Rothstein, 1990).

The third phase historically coincides with the process of industrialization. As laid out in the classic account of Polanyi (1944), with capitalist development, ordinary people face new types of risk. New organizations emerge to provide what are initially discretionary welfare benefits – to the extent the fiscal resources permit – for ideological or electoral reasons. These groups may be political parties, charitable societies, or trade unions. They fill the void created by the shift of the population out of agricultural production in conjunction with inadequate government services due to the latter's insufficient extractive capacity to redistribute and mitigate risk (cf. Barr, 2001). In many developing countries today, even though similar bespoke organizations do not exist or are too weak to take on this burden, the demand for welfare clientelism is still present. We find traces of this phase in the empirical work conducted in Argentina that is reported in Stokes et al. (2013). But rather than undertaken by ideologically oriented political parties or similar programmatic organizations, as was the case in Europe, contemporary welfare clientelism is the purview of personalistic political parties, such as the Peronists in Argentina (Auyero, 2000), or of repurposed traditional authority structures, such as the informal nonpartisan broker structures found in Indonesia and the Philippines (Aspinall & Hicken, 2020) or the religious organizations reported in India (Thachil, 2014).

In the absence of a formal welfare state, the distorted and discretionary provisions that are made by individual politicians and political parties may still be better than nothing (Hicken, 2011). Welfare clientelism, however, is far from the ideal of universal, equitable, and fair entitlement. It distorts who receives benefits. It is also far from efficient in the delivery of public goods due to the lack of professional bureaucratic structures to do so. Not surprisingly, as a country becomes richer, (some) voters campaign for changes. In the case of Argentina, Weitz-Shapiro (2014) documents how middle-class voters used electoral competition between parties to extract promises of state reforms and an expansion of the state bureaucracy. In the case of the United Kingdom and the United States, business groups pressed for the introduction of a meritocratic civil service and the shift from nonprogrammatic to programmatic party politics (Kuo, 2018). Sometimes programmatic policies are implemented to reduce the popularity of political opponents, the most famous example being Otto von Bismark's creation of unemployment insurance in 1889 – the first in the world – in part aimed at undercutting the political support of workers that the German Social Democratic Party's successful welfare clientelism had generated.

When these reforms cumulate successfully, clientelism enters its fourth phase, one characterized by the last remnants of discretionary political disbursements that remain in the polities of the wealthy world. In this world, the gift-giving that was once part and parcel of campaign clientelism is transformed into mass advertising. Welfare clientelism is replaced largely by programmatic policies, but modest forms of discretionary spending remain, if only to permit politicians to credit claim during their electoral campaigns. Overall, two key changes are worth noting. First, politicians are forced to respond to voters' needs rather than using funds exclusively for their own electoral advantage.[23] The partisanship that may have characterized the distribution of services to individual voters evaporates, as elected representatives instead engage in nonpartisan constituency service to help voters trace a lost unemployment check, register to vote, or decipher the rules of a government program (Cain et al., 1987). Second, clientelism adapts to the routinization of policies that characterizes the world's wealthy democracies. Development funds disappear. Legislators include local public good projects for their constituencies within bigger pieces of legislation. Pork-barrel politics in some cases are used to grease the wheels that make the political system work (Evans, 2004). Such disbursements are no longer pure clientelism, since legislators no longer have full discretion over the relevant budget, but they are descendants of genuine clientelism.

6.2 Possible Avenues for Future Research

In this Element, we have reviewed a large literature, one that has made enormous progress in unpacking the operation and functioning of clientelism. Scholars have studied the relationship between candidates and their brokers. Likewise, they have investigated whether core or swing voters receive more benefits of campaign clientelism. And they have puzzled over how politicians enforce what appear to be clientelist exchanges. But to our mind, attending to

---

[23] An interesting study of the historical growth of pork-barrel politics for credit claiming purposes may be found in Gordon and Simpson (2018). Also relevant are Grimmer (2013) and Grimmer et al. (2014), which study how legislators in the United States communicate local public goods achievements to their constituents.

the dynamics of how clientelism operates is a narrow a research agenda that fails to exploit the full scope of the perspective introduced by Stokes et al. (2013). Reinvigorating modernization theory, that study offers some broad hypotheses about the demise of clientelism, mainly involving economic development and the increasing scale of modern society. In our view, empirical investigations of the demise of clientelism represent an essential next step for students of developing democracies. Increasingly, research in developing democracies finds evidence that clientelism, although still obvious, is no longer the sole or predominant mode of political engagement for citizens. Instead, it is being displaced by constituency service: the routinized, nonpartisan assistance that politicians supply voters to help manage interactions with government bureaucracies (Bussell, 2019; Golden et al., 2021). We suspect that we would learn a great deal if field researchers widened their purview to explicitly incorporate instances of interactions between politicians and citizens that were not clientelistic alongside those that are.

Another way to investigate the demise of clientelism is to focus on the recent anti-corruption movements that we referenced above. Under what conditions do they emerge? When are they successful, and what forms does success assume? What are the characteristics of the voters they appeal to, and on what grounds are appeals made? Are they capable of overturning clientelistic practices or do they get caught up in them as they navigate the corridors of power? These are key questions on which we await research.

New anti-clientelist political parties often recruit new and untested candidates to run for public office. Understanding this requires a better understanding of who has the incentive to run with a new and inexperienced political party. There is now a burgeoning literature on who becomes a politician, recently reviewed in Gulzar (2021). But there is still much work to be done to understand who politicians are, how they differ from the citizens they represent, and how a professionalized political class emerges. Comparative and historical research on the issue is also called for, along the lines of Thompson et al. (2019), which provides an analysis of the supply of politicians in the United States after World War II. How does the pool of politicians change as countries develop? When do voters insist that politicians put an end to clientelism, and when and how do they elect politicians who are able to do that?

A final avenue for future research arises out of the new data that we have presented on reelection rates around the world. These data are, to the best of our knowledge, the most extensive reelection data on individual politicians available. They provide the first systematic documentation corroborating the suspicion raised by prior studies that reelection rates in less developed countries are much lower, on average, than those in the world's wealthy nations.

Of course, we want to know why this is the case. At the level of individual politicians, we want to know more about the incentives and motives of those who win a seat in the national legislature in a less developed country only to lose office after a single term. Such persons represent the overwhelming majority of national legislators in the world's low- and middle-income countries. Presumably they are aware, even before entering office, that their chances of gaining reelection are low. How does this affect their behavior in office? Do they try to run again, or do they withdraw voluntarily from political competition after a single term? Why enter the national parliament if it does not foreshadow a lengthy political career, as occurs in the world's wealthy nations? All of political science research into legislative politics and lawmaking assumes that politicians seek above all to remain in office indefinitely (Mayhew, 1974); removing this assumption alters all the incentives for politicians – as well as any ability of voters to hold them to account for poor performance. How much of the difference in politics that we observe across nations may be linked to differences in the career trajectories of national politicians? These questions await new research.

Appendix I
Data Definitions

Clientelism: V-Dem Clientelism Index (v2xnp_client), 2012: "To what extent are politics based on clientelistic relationships?" (Coppedge et al., 2022, p. 295; Sigman & Lindberg, 2018).

Party institutionalization: V-Dem Party Institutionalization Index (v2xps_party), 2012: "To what extent are political parties institutionalized?" (Coppedge et al., 2022, p. 315; Bizzaro et al., 2017).

District magnitude: Lower chamber election district magnitude (v2elloeldm) as of 2012: "For this election, what was the average district magnitude for seats in the lower (or unicameral) chamber of the legislature?" (Coppedge et al., 2022, p. 78). Austria, Singapore, and Venezuela are missing from V-Dem for 2012; we use the 2013 value for Austria and the 2015 values for Singapore and Venezuela.

GDP: GDP per capita estimates from 2012 at purchasing power parity (in 2011 prices).

Reelection rates: Reelection rates calculated using data on the reentry of individual legislators into the lower house of representatives between 2000 and 2018. Data cover 98 countries and multiple elections for 51 of them. Measure used is country averages of individual legislator reentry into the next legislature. We consider a legislator reelected if she was elected at time t in constituency i, conditional on her election in the same or a different constituency at time $(t - 1)$. If a legislator skipped a legislature, we do not consider her reelected.

Appendix II
Data Sources

Clientelism, Party Institutionalization, District Magnitude:

- Coppedge, Michael, John Gerring, Carl Henrik Knutsen, Staffan I. Lindberg, Jan Teorell, Nazifa Alizada, David Altman, Michael Bernhard, Agnes Cornell, M. Steven Fish, Lisa Gastaldi, Haakon Gjerløw, Adam Glynn, Sandra Grahn, Allen Hicken, Garry Hindle, Nina Ilchenko, Katrin Kinzelbach, Joshua Krusell, Kyle L. Marquardt, Kelly McMann, Valeriya Mechkova, Juraj Medzihorsky, Pamela Paxton, Daniel Pemstein, Josefine Pernes, Oskar Ryden, Johannes von Römer, Brigitte Seim, Rachel Sigman, Svend-Erik Skaaning, Jeffrey Staton, Aksel Sundström, Eitan Tzelgov, Yi-ting Wang, Tore Wig, Steven Wilson and Daniel Ziblatt. 2022. "V-Dem [Country-Year/Country-Date] Dataset v12 Varieties of Democracy (V-Dem) Project." https://doi.org/10.23696/vdemds22
- Pemstein, Daniel, Kyle L. Marquardt, Eitan Tzelgov, Yi-ting Wang, Juraj Medzihorsky, Joshua Krusell, Farhad Miri, and Johannes von Römer. 2022. "The V-Dem Measurement Model: Latent Variable Analysis for Cross-National and Cross-Temporal Expert-Coded Data." V-Dem Working Paper No. 21. 7th edition. University of Gothenburg: Varieties of Democracy Institute.
- The V-Dem v12 data are accessed via the R vdemdata package (as of March 2022): Maerz, Seraphine F., Amanda B. Edgell, Sebastian Hellemeier, and Nina Illchenko. 2022. vdemdata: An R package to load, explore and work with the most recent V-Dem (Varieties of Democracy) dataset. https://github.com/vdeminstitute/vdemdata (last accessed in June 2022)

GDP: World Bank 2012. https://data.worldbank.org/indicator/NY.GDP.PCAP.PP.KD (accessed in July 8, 2017).

Reelection rates:

CLEA: Kollman, Ken, Allen Hicken, Daniele Caramani, David Backer, and David Lublin. Constituency-Level Elections Archive (CLEA). Ann Arbor, MI: Center for Political Studies, University of Michigan [producer and distributor], 2018. www.electiondataarchive.org/datacenter.html. Release: 19 November 2018 (accessed November 27, 2018).

Everypolitician: EveryPolitician open-source dataset on politicians. http://everypolitician.org (last accessed in November 2018).

Parliamentary website: Official website of the national parliament (see details under the list of countries below).

Psephos: Adam Carr's electoral archive. http://psephos.adam-carr.net (last accessed in 2018).

Wikipedia: The lists of elected legislators from Wikipedia (see details under the list of countries below).

List of data sources and legislative election years by country (the first election year for each country is dropped when reelection rates are calculated):

1. Afghanistan: 2005 from CLEA, 2010 from parliamentary website, http://wolesi.website/pve/page.aspx?Cat=101 (accessed November 24, 2018)
2. Albania: 2009 and 2013 from Everypolitician
3. Angola: 2012 and 2017 from Everypolitician
4. Armenia: 2012 and 2017 from Everypolitician
5. Australia: 1998, 2001, 2004, 2007, 2010, 2013, 2016 from Everypolitician
6. Austria: 1999, 2002, 2006, 2008, 2013, 2017 from parliamentary website, https://www.parlament.gv.at/WWER/PARL/
7. Azerbaijan: 2010 and 2015 from Everypolitician
8. Bangladesh: 2008 from Wikipedia (accessed June 6, 2022) and 2014 from parliamentary website www.parliament.gov.bd/index.php/en/mps/members-of-parliament/former-mp-s/list-of-10th-parliament-members-english (accessed June 6, 2022)
9. Belarus: 2012 and 2016 from Everypolitician
10. Belgium: 1999, 2003, 2007, 2010, 2014 from parliamentary website, www.dekamer.be (accessed December 8, 2018)
11. Botswana: 2009 from Wikipedia (accessed November 26, 2018), 2014 from Everypolitician
12. Brazil: 2002, 2006, 2010, 2014 from parliamentary website, www2.camara.leg.br/transparencia/dados-abertos/dados-abertos-legislativo/webservices/deputadosr (accessed June 28, 2022)
13. Bulgaria: 2001, 2005, 2009, 2013, 2014, 2017 from Everypolitician
14. Burkina Faso: 2012 and 2015 from Everypolitician
15. Burundi: 2010 and 2015 from Everypolitician
16. Cabo Verde: 2011 and 2016 from Everypolitician
17. Cambodia: 2013 from Everypolitician, 2018 from parliamentary website, www.nac.org.kh/group-article/115 (Google translated, accessed November 7, 2018)
18. Cameroon: 1997, 2002, 2007, 2013. Yonatan L. Morse, 2021, Replication data ("Biographical Dataset of Cameroonian Legislators") for: "The Legislature as Political Control: Change and Continuity in Cameroon's National Assembly (1973-2019)," https://doi.org/10.1017/S0022278X2

1000288 downloaded from https://sites.google.com/site/yonatanmorse/home/data-1?authuser=0 on June 29, 2022.

19. Canada: 1997, 2000, 2004, 2006, 2008, 2011, 2015 from parliamentary website, www.ourcommons.ca (accessed December 7, 2018)
20. Chile: 1997, 2001, 2005, 2009, 2013 from Everypolitician
21. Colombia: 2006, 2010 from Psephos
22. Cote d'Ivoire: 2011 from Everypolitician, 2016 from Psephos
23. Croatia: 2000, 2003, 2007, 2011, 2015, 2016 from parliamentary website, www.sabor.hr/en/mps (accessed August 14, 2022)
24. Cyprus: 2011 and 2016 from Everypolitician
25. Czech Republic: 2002, 2006, 2010, 2013 from parliamentary website, www.psp.cz (accessed December 7, 2018)
26. Denmark: 1998, 2001, 2005, 2007, 2011, 2015 from Everypolitician
27. El Salvador: 2015 from Everypolitician, 2018 from Psephos
28. Estonia: 2011 and 2015 Everypolitician
29. Finland: 1999, 2003, 2007, 2011, 2015 from Everypolitician
30. France: 2002, 2007, 2012, 2017 from Everypolitician
31. Gambia: 2007, 2011, 2017 from CLEA
32. Georgia: 2012 and 2016 from Everypolitician
33. Germany: 1998, 2002, 2005, 2009, 2013, 2017 from Everypolitician
34. Ghana: 2012 and 2016 from Everypolitician
35. Greece: 1996, 2000, 2004, 2007, 2009, 2012 (two legislative elections in May and June 2012), 2015 (two legislative elections in January and September 2015) from Everypolitician
36. Guatemala: 2011 and 2015 from Everypolitician
37. Hungary: 2014 and 2018 from Everypolitician
38. Iceland: 1999, 2003, 2007, 2009, 2013 from Everypolitician
39. India: 1999, 2004, 2009, 2014 from parliamentary website, http://164.100.47.194/Loksabha/Members/lokprev.aspx (accessed November 23, 2018)
40. Indonesia: 2009 and 2014 from CLEA
41. Iran: 1996, 2000, 2004, 2008. Paasha Mahdavi, 2015, "Replication data for: Explaining the Oil Advantage: Effects of Natural Resource Wealth on Incumbent Reelection in Iran," https://doi.org/10.7910/DVN/28583, Harvard Dataverse, V1 (accessed December 3, 2018)
42. Ireland: 1997, 2002, 2007, 2011, 2016 from Everypolitician
43. Israel: 1999, 2003, 2006, 2009, 2013, 2015 from Everypolitician
44. Italy: 1996, 2001, 2006, 2008, 2013, 2018 from parliamentary website, http://documenti.camera.it/apps/nuovosito/deputato/ricercadeputato/risultato.asp?selezione=A (accessed September 27, 2018)
45. Jamaica: 2002, 2007, 2011, 2016 from CLEA

46. Japan: 2014 and 2017 from Everypolitician
47. Kazakhstan: 2007, 2012, 2016 from Wikipedia
48. Kenya: 2013 and 2017 from parliamentary website, www.parliament.go
    .ke (accessed December 8, 2018) (10th and 11th legislatures were retrieved
    from the snapshots of the official website via web.archive.org dated March
    13, 2013, and April 26, 2013 respectively)
49. Kosovo: 2001, 2004, 2007, 2010, 2014 from Everypolitician
50. Kyrgyzstan: 2010 and 2015 from Everypolitician
51. Latvia: 2010, 2011, 2014 from Everypolitician
52. Lebanon: 2009 from Everypolitician, 2018 from Wikipedia (accessed
    December 7, 2018)
53. Lesotho: 2015 and 2017 from CLEA
54. Liberia: 2011 and 2017 from CLEA
55. Lithuania: 1996, 2000, 2004, 2008, 2012, 2016 from parliamentary web-
    site, www.lrs.lt/sip/portal.show?p_r=35357&p_k=2 (accessed June 1,
    2022)
56. Luxembourg: 1999, 2004, 2009, 2013 from CLEA
57. Malawi: 2004, 2009, 2014 from CLEA
58. Malaysia: 1999, 2004, 2008, 2013 from Everypolitician
59. Maldives: 2009 and 2014 from CLEA
60. Malta: 1998, 2003, 2008, 2013, 2017 from parliamentary website, https:
    //parlament.mt/en/14th-leg/political-groups/ (accessed August 16, 2022)
61. Mauritius: 2010 and 2014 from CLEA
62. Mongolia: 2008, 2012, 2016 from Everypolitician
63. Myanmar: 2010 and 2015 from CLEA
64. Namibia: 1999, 2004, 2009, 2014 from Everypolitician
65. Netherlands: 2012 from parliamentary website www.houseofrepresenta
    tives.nl/members_of_parliament/members_of_parliament (the 2012 leg-
    islature retrieved from the snapshot of the official website via
    web.archive.org dated January 21, 2013; accessed August 14, 2022) and
    2017 from Everypolitician
66. New Zealand: 2005, 2008, 2011, 2014, 2017 from Everypolitician
67. Nigeria: 2011 from CLEA, 2007 from Psephos
68. Norway: 1997, 2001, 2005, 2009, 2013, 2017. Fiva, J. H. and D. M. Smith
    (2022): "Norwegian Parliamentary Elections, 1906–2021" (version 2022),
    downloaded from Jon H. Fiva's website www.jon.fiva.no/data/FivaSmith
    2022.zip on August 16, 2022.
69. Pakistan: 2002 and 2008 from CLEA, 2013 from parliamentary website,
    www.na.gov.pk/en/all$_m$embers.php (accessed Fall 2017)

70. Peru: 2000, 2001, 2006, 2011, 2016 from parliamentary website, www .congreso.gob.pe/eng (accessed March 20, 2019)
71. Philippines: 2013 and 2016 from Everypolitician
72. Poland: 1997, 2001, 2005, 2007, 2011, 2015 from Everypolitician
73. Portugal: 1999, 2002, 2005, 2009, 2011, 2015 from Everypolitician
74. Romania: 2012 and 2016 from Everypolitician
75. Russia: 2003, 2007, 2011, 2016 from parliamentary website, www.duma .gov.ru/ (accessed Fall 2017)
76. Serbia: 2014 and 2016 from Everypolitician
77. Sierra Leone: 2012 from Everypolitician, 2018 from Psephos
78. Singapore: 1997, 2001, 2006, 2011, 2015 from Everypolitician
79. Slovakia: 1998, 2002, 2006, 2010, 2012, 2016 from Everypolitician
80. Slovenia: 2014 and 2018 from Everypolitician
81. Solomon Islands: 2006, 2010, 2014 from CLEA
82. South Korea: 2012 and 2016 from Everypolitician
83. Spain: 2000, 2004, 2008, 2011, 2016 from parliamentary website www.congreso.es/en/busqueda-de-diputados (accessed August 14, 2022)
84. Suriname: 2010 and 2015 from Everypolitician
85. Sweden: 1998, 2002, 2006, 2010, 2014 from Everypolitician
86. Switzerland: 1999, 2003, 2007, 2011, 2015 from Everypolitician
87. Tanzania: 2000, 2005, 2010, 2015 from Everypolitician
88. Togo: 2013 from Everypolitician, 2007 from Psephos
89. Trinidad and Tobago: 2015 from Everypolitician, 2010 from Psephos
90. Turkey: 1999, 2002, 2007, 2011, 2015 (two legislative elections in June and November 2015) from Everypolitician
91. Turkmenistan: 2008 and 2013 from Everypolitician
92. Uganda: 2011 and 2016 from Everypolitician
93. United Kingdom: 1997, 2001, 2005, 2010, 2015, 2017 from Everypolitician
94. Ukraine: 1998, 2002, 2006, 2007, 2012, 2014, 2019 from parliamentary website, https://data.rada.gov.ua/open/data/mps-all (accessed August 18, 2020)
95. United States: 1998, 2000, 2002, 2004, 2006, 2008, 2010, 2012, 2014, 2016. Candidate-level dataset of U.S. Federal House election returns from 1870 to 2016. Provided directly to us by James Snyder.
96. Venezuela: 2010 and 2015 from Everypolitician
97. Zambia: 2011 and 2016 from Everypolitician
98. Zimbabwe: 2013 from Everypolitician, 2018 from the list of MPs and Senators declared elected after July 30, 2018, harmonized elections http://veritaszim.net/node/3107 (accessed November 20, 2018)

References

Akhmedov, A., & Zhuravskaya, E. (2004). Opportunistic political cycles: Test in a young democracy setting. *The Quarterly Journal of Economics*, *119*(4), 1301–38.

Aldrich, J. (1995). *Why parties? The origin and transformation of political parties in America*. Chicago: University of Chicago Press.

Arias, E., Balán, P., Larreguy, H., Marshall, J., & Querubín, P. (2019). Information provision, voter coordination, and electoral accountability: Evidence from Mexican social networks. *American Political Science Review*, *113*(2), 475–98.

Aspinall, E., & Berenschot, W. (2019). *Democracy for sale: Elections, clientelism, and the state in Indonesia*. Ithaca, NY: Cornell University Press.

Aspinall, E., & Hicken, A. (2020). Guns for hire and enduring machines: Clientelism beyond parties in Indonesia and the Philippines. *Democratization*, *27*(1), 137–56.

Aspinall, E., Rohman, N., Hamdi, A. Z., & Triantini, Z. E. (2017). Vote buying in Indonesia: Candidate strategies, market logic and effectiveness. *Journal of East Asian Studies*, *17*(1), 1–27.

Asunka, J. (2017). Non-discretionary resource allocation as political investment: Evidence from Ghana. *Journal of Modern African Studies*, *55*(1), 29–53.

Auerbach, A. M., & Thachil, T. (2018). How clients select brokers: Competition and choice in India's slums. *American Political Science Review*, *112*(4), 775–91.

Auyero, J. (2000). *Poor people's politics: Peronist survival networks and the legacy of Evita*. New York: Duke University Press.

Avis, E., Ferraz, C., & Finan, F. (2018). Do government audits reduce corruption? Estimating the impacts of exposing corrupt politicians. *Journal of Political Economy*, *126*(5), 1912–64.

Bailey, F. (1963). *Politics and social change: Orissa in 1959*. Berkeley: University of California Press.

Baland, J.- M., & Robinson, J. A. (2008, December). Land and power: Theory and evidence from Chile. *American Economic Review*, *98*(5), 1737–65.

Banerjee, A., Kumar, S., Pande, R., & Su, F. (2011). Do informed voters make better choices? Experimental evidence from urban India. (Unpublished manuscript).

Barr, N. (2001). *The welfare state as piggy bank: Information, risk, uncertainty, and the role of the state.* Oxford: Oxford University Press.

Berenschot, W. (2010). Everyday mediation: The politics of public service delivery in Gujarat, India. *Development and Change, 41*(5), 883–905.

Berry, C. R., Burden, B. C., & Howell, W. G. (2010). The president and the distribution of federal spending. *American Political Science Review, 104*(4), 783–99.

Bhandari, A., Marshall, J., & Larreguy, H. (in press). Able and mostly willing: An empirical anatomy of information's effect on voter-driven accountability in Senegal. *American Journal of Political Science.*

Bizzarro, F., Hicken, A., & Self, D. (2017). *The V-Dem party institutionalization index: A new global indicator (1900–2015)* (Working Paper No. 48). V-Dem Institute, University of Gothenburg.

Blattman, C., Larreguy, H., Marx, B., & Reid, O. R. (2019, September). *Eat widely, vote wisely? Lessons from a campaign against vote buying in Uganda* (Working Paper No. 26293). National Bureau of Economic Research.

Bowles, J., & Marx, B. (2022). Turnover and accountability in Africa's parliaments (Unpublished paper).

Brass, P. R. (1965). *Factional politics in an Indian state: The Congress Party in Uttar Pradesh.* Berkeley: University of California Press.

Bratton, M. (2008, December). Vote buying and violence in Nigerian election campaigns. *Electoral Studies, 27*(4), 621–32.

Brierley, S., & Nathan, N. L. (2021). The connections of party brokers: Which brokers do parties select? *Journal of Politics, 83*(3), 884–901.

Brierley, S., & Nathan, N. L. (2022). Motivating the machine: Which brokers do parties pay? *Journal of Politics,* 84(3), 1539–1555

Bussell, J. (2019). *Clients and constituents: Political responsiveness in patronage democracies.* New York, NY: Oxford University Press.

Cain, B., Ferejohn, J., & Fiorina, M. (1987). *The personal vote: Constituency service and electoral independence.* Cambridge, MA: Harvard University Press.

Calvo, E., & Murillo, M. V. (2004, October). Who delivers? Partisan clients in the Argentine electoral market. *American Journal of Political Science, 48*(4), 742–57.

Canes-Wrone, B., & Park, J.-K. (2012, February). Electoral business cycles in OECD countries. *American Political Science Review, 106*(1), 103–22.

Cantú, F. (2019, July). Groceries for votes: The electoral returns of vote buying. *Journal of Politics, 81*(3), 790–804.

Carey, J. M. (1996). *Term limits and legislative representation.* Cambridge: Cambridge University Press.

Carey, J. M., & Shugart, M. S. (1995). Incentives to cultivate a personal vote: A rank ordering of electoral formulas. *Electoral Studies, 14,* 417–39.

Carlin, R. E., & Moseley, M. W. (2021). When clientelism backfires: Vote buying, democratic attitudes, and electoral retaliation in Latin America. *Political Research Quarterly, 75*(3), 766–781.

Carlitz, R. (2017, May). Money flows, water trickles: Understanding patterns of decentralized water provision in Tanzania. *World Development, 93,* 16–30.

Casas, A. (2018). Distributive politics with vote and turnout buying. *American Political Science Review, 112*(4), 1111–19.

Caselli, M., & Falco, P. (in press). Your vote is (no) secret! How low voter density hurts anonymity and biases elections in Italy. *European Journal of Political Economy, 75.*

Catalinac, A., & Muraoka, T. (2021). Programmatic policies increase the clientelistic goods received by policy beneficiaries (Unpublished paper).

Chandra, K. (2004). *Why ethnic parties succeed: Patronage and ethnic head counts in India.* Cambridge: Cambridge University Press.

Chandra, K. (2007). Counting heads: A theory of voter and elite behavior in patronage democracies. In H. Kitschelt & S. I. Wilkinson (Eds.), *Patrons, clients, and policies: Patterns of democratic accountability and political competition* (pp. 84–109). Cambridge: Cambridge University Press.

Chang, E. C., Golden, M. A., & Hill, S. J. (2010, April). Legislative malfeasance and political accountability. *World Politics, 62*(2), 177–220.

Chauchard, S. (2018). Electoral handouts in Mumbai elections: The cost of political competition. *Asian Survey, 58,* 341–64.

Chubb, J. (1982). *Patronage, power and poverty in Southern Italy: A tale of two cities.* Cambridge: Cambridge University Press.

Coate, S., & Morris, S. (1999, December). Policy persistence. *American Economic Review, 89*(5), 1327–36.

Colonnelli, E., Prem, M., & Teso, E. (2020). Patronage and selection in public sector organizations. *American Economic Review, 110*(10), 3071–99.

Coppedge, M., Gerring, J., Knutsen, C. H. et al. (2022, March). *V-Dem codebook v12* (Working Paper). V-Dem Institute, University of Gothenburg. https://www.v-dem.net/static/website/img/refs/codebookv12.pdf

Cox, G. W., & Kousser, J. M. (1981, November). Turnout and rural corruption: New York as a test case. *American Journal of Political Science, 25*(4), 646–63.

Cruz, C. (2019). Social networks and the targeting of vote buying. *Comparative Political Studies, 52*(3), 382–411.

Cruz, C., Keefer, P., & Labonne, J. (2021, April). Buying informed voters: New effects of information on voters and candidates. *Economic Journal, 131*(635), 1105–34.

Cruz, C., Keefer, P., Labonne, J., & Trebbi, F. (2018, June). *Making policies matter: Voter responses to campaign promises* (Working Paper, No. 24785). National Bureau of Economic Research.

Dewan, T., & Shepsle, K. A. (2011). Political economy models of elections. *Annual Review of Political Science, 14*, 311–30.

Diaz-Cayeros, A., Estévez, F., & Magaloni, B. (2016). *The political logic of poverty relief: Electoral strategies and social policy in Mexico.* New York: Cambridge University Press.

Diaz-Cayeros, A., Magaloni, B., & Estévez, F. (2007). Clientelism and portfolio diversification: A model of electoral investment with applications to Mexico. In H. Kitschelt (Ed.), *Patrons, clients, and policies: Patterns of democratic accountability and political competition* (pp. 182–205). New York: Cambridge University Press.

Dixit, A., & Londregan, J. (1996, November). The determinants of success of special interests in redistributive politics. *Journal of Politics, 58*(4), 1132–55.

Dunning, T., Grossman, G., Humphreys, M., Hyde, S., & McIntosh, C. (Eds.). (2019). *Information and accountability: A new method for cumulative learning.* New York: Cambridge University Press.

Eater. (2020). *If you feed them, will they vote?* www.eater.com/2020/2/18/21140518/mike-bloomberg-campaign-spending-free-food-voting-democrat-primary.

Eggers, A. C., & Spirling, A. (2017). Incumbency effects and the strength of party preferences: Evidence from multiparty elections in the United Kingdom. *Journal of Politics, 79*(3), 903–20.

Evans, D. (2004). *Greasing the wheels: Using pork barrel projects to build majority coalitions in Congress.* Cambridge: Cambridge University Press.

Fearon, J. D. (1999). Electoral accountability and the control of politicians: Selecting good types versus sanctioning poor performance. In A. Przeworski, S. C. Stokes, & B. Manin (Eds.), *Democracy, accountability, and representation* (pp. 55–97). New York: Cambridge University Press.

Ferejohn, J. A. (1974). *Pork barrel politics: Rivers and harbors legislation, 1947–1968.* Stanford: Stanford University Press.

Ferraz, C., & Finan, F. (2008, May). Exposing corrupt politicians: The effect of Brazil's publicly released audits on electoral outcomes. *Quarterly Journal of Economics, 123*(2), 703–45.

Ferree, K. F., & Long, J. D. (2016, October). Gifts, threats, and perceptions of ballot secrecy in African elections. *African Affairs, 115*(461), 621–45.

Finan, F., & Schechter, L. (2012, March). Vote-buying and reciprocity. *Econometrica, 80*(2), 863–81.

Fisman, R., & Golden, M. A. (2017). *Political corruption: What everyone needs to know*. New York: Oxford University Press.

Fisman, R., Schultz, F., & Vig, V. (2014). Private returns to public office. *Journal of Political Economy, 122*(4), 806–62.

Fox, J. (1994). The difficult transition from clientelism to citizenship: Lessons from Mexico. *World Politics, 6*(2), 151–84.

Fox, J. (2015). Social accountability: What does the evidence really say? *World Development, 72*, 346–61.

Gagliarducci, S., & Nannicini, T. (2013, April). Do better paid politicians perform better? Disentangling incentives from selection. *Journal of the European Economic Association, 11*(3), 369–98.

Galasso, V., & Nannicini, T. (2011, February). Competing on good politicians. *American Political Science Review, 105*(1), 79–99.

Gans-Morse, J., Mazzuca, S., & Nichter, S. (2014). Varieties of clientelism: Machine politics during elections. *American Journal of Political Science, 58*(2), 415–32.

Geddes, B. (1994). *Politician's dilemma: Building state capacity in Latin America*. Berkeley: University of California Press.

Gerber, A. D., Huber, G. A., Doherty, D., & Dowling, C. M. (2013, January). Is there a secret ballot? Ballot secrecy perceptions and their implications for voting behavior. *British Journal of Political Science, 43*(1), 77–102.

Glaeser, E. L., & Goldin, C. (Eds.). (2006). *Corruption and reform: Lessons from America's economic history*. Chicago: University of Chicago Press.

Golden, M. A. (2003, April). Electoral connections: The effects of the personal vote on political patronage, bureaucracy and legislation in postwar Italy. *British Journal of Political Science, 33*(2), 189–212.

Golden, M. A., Gulzar, S., & Sonnet, L. (2021, September). "Press 1 for Roads": Improving political communication with new technology (Unpublished paper).

Golden, M. A., & Min, B. (2013). Distributive politics around the world. *Annual Review of Political Science, 16*, 73–99.

Golden, M. A., & Picci, L. (2015, November). Incumbency effects under proportional representation: Leaders and backbenchers in the postwar Italian chamber of deputies. *Legislative Studies Quarterly, 40*(4), 509–38.

Gonzalez-Ocantos, E., de Jonge, C. K., Meléndez, C., Nickerson, D., & Osorio, J. (2020). Carrots and sticks: Experimental evidence of vote-buying and voter intimidation in Latin America. *Journal of Peace Research*, *57*(1), 46–61.

Gonzalez-Ocantos, E., Kiewit de Jonge, C., Meléndez, C., Osorio, J., & Nickerson, D. W. (2012). Vote buying and social desirability bias: Experimental evidence from Nicaragua. *American Journal of Political Science*, *56*(1), 202–17.

Gordon, S. C. (2011). Politicizing agency spending authority: Lessons from a Bush-era scandal. *American Political Science Review*, *105*(4), 717–34.

Gordon, S. C., & Simpson, H. K. (2018). The birth of pork: Local appropriations in America's first century. *American Political Science Review*, *112*(3), 564–79.

Gottlieb, J., & Larreguy, H. (2020). An informational theory of electoral targeting in young clientelistic democracies: Evidence from Senegal. *Quarterly Journal of Political Science*, *15*, 1–32.

Grimmer, J. (2013). *Representational style in Congress: What legislators say and why it matters*. New York: Cambridge University Press.

Grimmer, J., Westwood, S. J., & Messing, S. (2014). *The impression of influence: Legislator communication, representation, and democratic accountability*. Princeton: Princeton University Press.

Grossman, G. M., & Helpman, E. (2001). *Special interest politics*. Cambridge, MA: MIT Press.

Guardado, J., & Wantchekon, L. (2018). Do electoral handouts affect voting behavior? *Electoral Studies*, *53*, 139–49.

Guardado, J., & Wantchekon, L. (2021). *Do gifts buy votes? Evidence from sub-Saharan Africa* (Working Paper No. 129). United Nations University World Institute for Development Economics Research.

Gulzar, S. (2021). Who enters politics and why? *Annual Review of Political Science*, *24*, 253–75.

Gutiérrez-Romero, R. (2014). An inquiry into the use of illegal electoral practices and effects of political violence and vote-buying. *Journal of Conflict Resolution*, *58*(8), 1500–27.

Hicken, A. (2011). Clientelism. *Annual Review of Political Science*, *14*, 289–310.

Hicken, A., & Nathan, N. L. (2020). Clientelism's red herrings: Dead ends and new directions in the study of nonprogrammatic politics. *Annual Review of Political Science*, *23*(1), 277–294.

Holland, A. C., & Palmer-Rubin, B. (2015). Beyond the machine: Clientelist brokers and interest organizations in Latin America. *Comparative Political Studies*, *48*(9), 1186–223.

Imai, K., King, G., & Velasco Rivera, C. (2020). Do nonpartisan programmatic policies have partisan electoral effects? Evidence from two large-scale experiments. *Journal of Politics*, *82*(2), 714–730.

Jain, A. K. (2001). Corruption: A review. *Journal of Economic Surveys*, *15*(1), 71–121.

Kam, C. (2017). The secret ballot and the market for votes in 19th-century British elections. *Comparative Political Studies*, *50*(5), 594–635.

Keefer, P., & Khemani, S. (2009, February). When do legislators pass on pork? The role of political parties in determining legislator effort. *American Political Science Review*, *103*(1), 99–112.

Keefer, P., & Vlaicu, R. (2008). Democracy, credibility, and clientelism. *Journal of Law, Economics, and Organization*, *24*(2), 371–406.

Key, V., Jr. (1935, March). Methods of evasion of civil service laws. *South-western Social Science Quarterly*, *15*(4), 337–47.

Khemani, S. (2004). Political cycles in a developing economy: Effect of elections in the Indian states. *Journal of Development Economics*, *73*, 125–54.

Kitschelt, H., & Wilkinson, S. I. (Eds.). (2007). *Patrons, clients, and policies: Patterns of democratic accountability and political competition.* Cambridge: Cambridge University Press.

Klašnja, M., & Titiunik, R. (2017). The incumbency curse: Weak parties, term limits, and unfulfilled accountability. *American Political Science Review*, *111*(1), 129–48.

Kramer, G. H. (1971, March). Short-term fluctuations in U.S. voting behavior, 1896–1964. *American Political Science Review*, *65*(1), 131–43.

Kramon, E. (2018). *Money for votes: The causes and consequences of electoral clientelism in Africa.* New York: Cambridge University Press.

Kruks-Wisner, G. (2018). *Claiming the state: Active citizenship and social welfare in rural India.* New York: Cambridge University Press.

Kuo, D. (2018). *Clientelism, capitalism, and democracy: The rise of programmatic politics in the United States and Britain.* New York: Cambridge University Press.

Larreguy, H., Marshall, J., & Snyder, J. M. (2020, October). Publicizing malfeasance: When the local media structure facilitates electoral accountability in Mexico. *Economic Journal*, *130*(631), 2291–327.

Lasswell, H. D. (1936). *Politics: Who gets what, when, how.* New York: McGraw-Hill.

Lawson, C., & Greene, K. F. (2014, October). Making clientelism work: How norms of reciprocity increase voter compliance. *Comparative Politics*, *47*(1), 61–85.

Lee, A. (2020, January). Incumbency, parties, and legislatures: Theory and evidence from India. *Comparative Politics, 52*(2), 311–31.

Lee, D. S. (2008). Randomized experiments from non-random selection in U.S. House elections. *Journal of Econometrics, 142*(2), 675–97.

Levitsky, S., & Way, L. (2010). *Competitive authoritarianism: Hybrid regimes after the Cold War*. New York: Cambridge University Press.

Lindberg, S. I. (2003, Summer). "It's our time to 'chop' ": Do elections in Africa feed neo-patrimonialism rather than counter-act it? *Democratization, 10*(2), 121–40.

Linden, L. L. (2004, January). Are incumbents really advantaged? The preference for non-incumbents in Indian national elections (Unpublished paper).

Magaloni, B. (2006). *Voting for autocracy: Hegemonic party survival and its demise in Mexico*. New York: Cambridge University Press.

Manion, M. (2004). *Corruption by design: Building clean government in mainland China and Hong Kong*. Cambridge, MA: Harvard University Press.

Mares, I. (2015). *From open secrets to secret ballots: The adoption of electoral reforms protecting voters against intimidation*. New York: Cambridge University Press.

Mares, I., & Young, L. E. (2018). The core voter's curse: Clientelistic threats and promises in Hungarian elections. *Comparative Political Studies, 51*(11), 1441–71.

Mares, I., & Young, L. E. (2019). *Conditionality and coercion: Electoral clientelism in Eastern Europe*. Oxford: Oxford University Press.

Martin, L., & Raffler, P. (2020, January). Fault lines: The effects of bureaucratic power on electoral accountability. *American Journal of Political Science, 65*(1), 210–24.

Mayhew, D. (1974). *Congress: The electoral connection*. New Haven, CT: Yale University Press.

Min, B., & Golden, M. (2014). Electoral cycles in electricity losses in India. *Energy Policy, 65*, 619–45.

Mohmand, S. K. (2019). *Crafty oligarchs, savvy voters: Democracy under inequality in rural Pakistan*. New York: Cambridge University Press.

Morgan, J., & Várdy, F. (2011). On the buyability of voting bodies. *Journal of Theoretical Politics, 23*(2), 260–87.

Morgan, J., & Várdy, F. (2012, October). Negative vote buying and the secret ballot. *Journal of Law, Economics, and Organization, 28*(4), 818–49.

Muhtadi, B. (2019). *Vote buying in Indonesia: The mechanics of electoral bribery*. Singapore: Palgrave Macmillan.

Muñoz, P. (2018). *Buying audiences: Clientelism and electoral campaigns when parties are weak*. New York: Cambridge University Press.

Nathan, N. (2019). *Electoral politics and Africa's urban transition: Class and ethnicity in Ghana*. New York: Cambridge University Press.

Nichter, S. (2008, February). Vote buying or turnout buying? Machine politics and the secret ballot. *American Political Science Review, 102*(1), 19–31.

Nichter, S. (2018). *Votes for survival: Relational clientelism in Latin America*. New York: Cambridge University Press.

Ohman, M. (2012). *Political finance regulations around the world: An overview of the international IDEA database* (Tech. Rep.). Stockholm: International Institute for Democracy and Electoral Assistance.

Oliveros, V. (2016). Making it personal: Clientelism, favors, and the personalization of public administration in Argentina. *Comparative Politics, 48*(3), 373–91.

Ostwald, K., & Riambau, G. (2017, June 15). Voting behavior under doubts of ballot secrecy (Unpublished paper).

Polanyi, K. (1944). *The great transformation: The political and economic origins of our time*. Boston: Beacon Press.

Prado, M. M. (2021). Using criminal law to fight corruption: The potential, risks and limitations of Operation Car Wash (Lava Jato). *American Journal of Comparative Law* 69(4), 834–879.

Przeworski, A. (2015). Suffrage and voting secrecy in general elections. In J. Elster (Ed.), *Secrecy and publicity in votes and debates* (pp. 97–107). New York: Cambridge University Press.

Przeworski, A., Alvarez, M. E., Cheibub, J. A., & Limongi, F. (2000). *Democracy and development: Political institutions and well-being in the world, 1950–1990*. New York: Cambridge University Press.

Querubin, P. (2012). Political reform and elite persistence: Term limits and political dynasties in the Philippines (Unpublished paper).

Rauschenbach, M., & Katin, P. (2019). Intimidating voters with violence and mobilizing them with clientelism. *Journal of Peace Research, 20*(10), 682–696.

Reynolds, A., & Steenbergen, M. (2006, September). How the world votes: The political consequences of ballot design, innovation and manipulation. *Electoral Studies, 25*(3), 570–98.

Robinson, J. A., & Verdier, T. (2013). The political economy of clientelism. *The Scandinavian Journal of Economics, 115*(2), 260–91.

Roth, G. (1963). *The social democrats in Imperial Germany: A study in working class isolation and national integration*. Totowa, NJ: Bedminster Press.

Rothstein, B. (1990). Marxism, institutional analysis and working-class power. *Politics & Society, 18*, 317–45.

Rueda, M. R. (2017, January). Small aggregates, big manipulation: Vote buying enforcement and collective monitoring. *American Journal of Political Science, 61*(1), 163–77.

Sáez, L., & Sinha, A. (2010). Political cycles, political institutions and public expenditure in India, 1980–2000. *British Journal of Political Science, 40*(1), 91–113.

Scanlon, T. (2018). *Why does inequality matter?* Oxford: Oxford University Press.

Schaffer, F. C. (2007). Lessons learned. In F. C. Schaffer (Ed.), *Elections for sale: The causes and consequences of vote buying* (pp. 253–281). Boulder, CO: Lynne Rienner.

Schaffer, J., & Baker, A. (2015). Clientelism as persuasion-buying: Evidence from Latin America. *Comparative Political Studies, 48*(9), 1093–126.

Schmidt, S. W., Guasti, L., Landé, C. H., & Scott, J. C. (Eds.). (1977). *Friends, followers, and factions: A reader in political clientelism.* Berkeley: University of California Press.

Schneider, M. (2020, October). Do local leaders know their voters? A test of guessability in India. *Electoral Studies, 61*, 102049.

Scott, J. C. (1972). *Comparative political corruption.* Englewood Cliffs, NJ: Prentice-Hall.

Sequeira, S. (2012). Advances in measuring corruption in the field. *New Advances in Experimental Research on Corruption (Research in Experimental Economics), 15*, 145–75.

Seymour, C. (1915). *Electoral reform in England and Wales: The development and operation of the parliamentary franchise, 1832–1885* (Vol. 3). New Haven: Yale University Press.

Shugart, M. S. (2005). The politics of electoral systems. In M. Gallagher & P. Mitchell (Eds.), *Comparative electoral systems research: The maturation of a field and the new challenges ahead* (pp. 25–55). Oxford: Oxford University Press.

Sigman, R. & Lindberg, S. I. (2018), Neopatrimonialism and Democracy: An Empirical Investigation of Africa's Political Regimes. in P. Von Doepp & G. Lynch (Eds.), *Handbook of Democratization in Africa* (pp. 17–37). London: Routledge.

Silverman, S. F. (1965, April). Patronage and community-nation relationships in central Italy. *Ethnology, 4*(2), 172–89.

Slough, T. (2021). Bureaucratic quality and the observability of electoral accountability (Unpublished paper).

Srinivas, M. (1955). The Social System of a Mysore Village. In M. Marriott (Ed.), Village India: Studies in the little community (pp. 1–35). Chicago: University of Chicago Press.

Stokes, S. C. (2005, August). Perverse accountability: A formal model of machine politics with evidence from Argentina. *American Political Science Review, 99*(3), 315–25.

Stokes, S. C., Dunning, T., Nazareno, M., & Brusco, V. (2013). *Brokers, voters, and clientelism: The puzzle of distributive politics.* New York: Cambridge University Press.

Szwarcberg, M. (2015). *Mobilizing poor voters: Machine politics, clientelism, and social networks in Argentina.* New York: Cambridge University Press.

Thachil, T. (2014). *Elite parties, poor voters: How social services win votes in India.* New York: Cambridge University Press.

Thompson, D. M., Feigenbaum, J. J., Hall, A. B., & Yoder, J. (2019, August). *Who becomes a member of Congress? Evidence from de-anonymized census data* (Working Paper No. 26156). National Bureau of Economic Research.

Trounstine, J. (2008). *Political monopolies in American cities: The rise and fall of bosses and reformers.* Chicago: University of Chicago Press.

Tufte, E. R. (1978). *Political control of the economy.* Princeton: Princeton University Press.

Uppal, Y. (2009). The disadvantaged incumbents: Estimating incumbency effects in Indian state legislatures. *Public Choice, 138*(1), 9–27.

Vasudevan, S. (2019, January). Diminishing the effectiveness of vote buying: Experimental evidence from a persuasive radio campaign in India (Unpublished paper).

Vicente, P. C. (2014, February). Is vote buying effective? Evidence from a field experiment in West Africa. *The Economic Journal, 124*(574), F356–F387.

Wantchekon, L. (2003, April). Clientelism and voting behavior: Evidence from a field experiment in Benin. *World Politics, 55*(3), 399–422.

Warren, S. S. (2019). Candidate selection and political accountability in African legislative elections (Unpublished doctoral dissertation). New York University.

Weingrod, A. (1968, July). Patrons, patronage, and political parties. *Comparative Studies in Society and History, 10*(4), 377–400.

Weitz-Shapiro, R. (2014). *Curbing clientelism in Argentina: Politics, poverty, and social policy.* New York: Cambridge University Press.

Wilder, A. R. (1999). *The Pakistani voter: Electoral politics and voting behaviour in the Punjab.* Oxford: Oxford University Press.

Williams, M. J. (2017). The political economy of unfinished development projects: Corruption, clientelism, or collective choice? *American Political Science Review, 111*(4), 705–23.

Wolf, E. R. (1966). Kinship, friendship, and patron-client relations in complex societies. In M. Banton (Ed.), *The social anthropology of complex societies* (pp. 1–22). London: Routledge.

Acknowledgments

The authors are grateful to David Stasavage for his skilled editorial guidance. We also thank Stephane Wolton for his intellectual contribution to this Element. For discussion of some of the ideas presented here, we acknowledge Manuel Bosancianu, Ana Garcia Hernandez, Anselm Hager, Hanno Hilbig, Macartan Humphreys, Heike Klüver, Liu Liu, Thomas Meyer, Alexandra Scacco, Kelly Zhang, and other participants at a book conference at the Wissenenschaftszentrum Berlin für Sozialforschung on February 27, 2020. We also received helpful readings from Alberto Diaz-Cayeros and Beatriz Magaloni. For research assistance, we thank Brian Hamel and Jonne Kamphorst. Funding for the data collection that is reported here was provided by the Academic Senate of the University of California at Los Angeles.

Cambridge Elements ☰

Political Economy

David Stasavage
New York University

David Stasavage is Julius Silver Professor in the Wilf Family Department of Politics at New York University. He previously held positions at the London School of Economics and at Oxford University. His work has spanned a number of different fields and currently focuses on two areas: development of state institutions over the long run and the politics of inequality. He is a member of the American Academy of Arts and Sciences.

About the Series

The Element Series Political Economy provides authoritative contributions on important topics in the rapidly growing field of political economy. Elements are designed so as to provide broad and in-depth coverage combined with original insights from scholars in political science, economics, and economic history. Contributions are welcome on any topic within this field.

Cambridge Elements ⁼

Political Economy

Elements in the Series

A full series listing is available at: www.cambridge.org/EPEC

Printed in the United States
by Baker & Taylor Publisher Services